MILLIONAIRE
FREELANCER

BEST WAYS TO MAKE MONEY FROM FREELANCE JOBS

MILLIONAIRE FREELANCER

Best Ways To Make Money From Freelance Jobs

By

Stephen Akintayo

Contents

ABOUT THE AUTHOR

Stephen Akintayo, is an inspirational speaker and Serial Entrepreneur. He is the Chief Executive Officer of *Stephen Akintayo Consulting International* and *Gtext Media* and *Investment Limited*, a leading firm in Nigeria whose services span from digital marketing, website design, bulk sms, online advertising, Media, e-commerce, real estate, Consulting and a host of other services.

He was born in Gonge Area of Maiduguri, Borno State in a very impoverished environment and with a civil Servant as a Mother who raised him and his four other siblings with her meagre salary since his father's contract business had crumbled. His humble beginnings contributed to his philanthrophic passion.

In his words; "Poverty was my surname. Hunger was my biggest challenge as a young boy. I had to scavenge through Elementary school to eat lunch. I didn't have lunch packs like other kids because we couldn't afford it. Things picked up in high school. Albeit, my mother still had to borrow money from her colleague to keep me in school each term. It was humiliating seeing their disdainful looks at my mum because of our constant begging. It hurt dearly. I hate Poverty and I strive to help more families come out of it".

Stephen Akintayo story is indeed a grass to grace one. It however saddens his heart that his hardworking mother died few years back due to ovarian cancer and never lived to see his successful endeavors and how much of a blessing he is to others.

Stephen, Also Founded *GileadBalm Group Services* which has assisted a number of businesses in Nigeria to move to enviable levels by helping them reach their clients through its enormous nationwide data base of real phone numbers and email addresses. It has hundreds of organizations as its clients including multinational companies like *Guaranty Trust Bank, PZ Cussons, MTN, Chivita,* among others.

He is also the Founder and President of two indigenous non-governmental organizations, *Infinity Foundation and Stephen Akintayo Foundation. Infinity Foundation* assists orphans and vulnerable children as well as mentor young minds. The foundation has assisted over 2,000 orphans and vulnerable children. It has also partnered with 22 orphanage homes in the country. In December 2015, *Infinity Foundation* launched *Mercy Orphanage* to care for victims and IDP's as a result of *Boko Haram* attacks in the Northern part of Nigeria.

The *Stephen Akintayo Foundation* gives out financial grants with 10 million Naira disbursed to 20 entrepreneurs during the pilot phase in 2015 and plans to grow that amount to 500 million naira annually by 2019. Other projects the foundation is involved in includes the *Upgrade Conference* and *The Serial Entrepreneur Conference* with thousands of attendees. The conferences are targetted at providing young entrepreneurs and career professionals an opportunity to learn and connect with excellent speakers, consultants and industry experts.

Also the founder of *Omonaija,* an online radio station in Lagos currently streaming for 24 hours daily with the capacity to reach every country of the world. As founder and director of *Digital Marketing School Nigeria*, Africa's leading digital marketing school, he is changing the narrative of digital marketing training with a very robust training curriculum. The school issues diploma certificates in Digital Marketing, Tele Marketing and Neuro Marketing.

Stephen is a media personality in the television, radio and print media. He anchors a programme on *Radio Continental,* tagged CEO Mentorship with Stephen Akintayo in addition to weekly column in some of Nigeria's national papers, including *The Nation Newspaper* and *The Union Newspapers.* He is also a social media guru.

His mentorship platform has helped thousands of people including graduates and undergraduates in the area of business as well as in building relationships. Stephen strongly believes young Nigerians with the passion for entrepreneurship can cause a business revolution in Nigeria and the world at large. He is a prolific writer and published author of several books including *Turning Your*

Mess To Message, Soul Mate, Survival Instincts and *Mobile Millionaire.*

A member of *The Institute of Strategic Management,* Stephen obtained his first degree in Microbiology from *Olabisi Onabanjo University.* He is a trained Digital Marketing Consultant by the *Digital Marketing Institute* at *Harvard University,* a trained coach by *The Coaching Academy UK* and he has several other professional training inside and outside Nigeria. Currently, he is running a Masters in Digital Marketing and MBA in Netherlands.

He is also an ordained Pastor with *Living Faith Church Worldwide* and is happily married and blessed with two sons; Divine Surprises and Future.

To invite Stephen Akintayo for a speaking engagement kindly email: invite@stephenakintayo.com or call:08188220066.

Copyright 2016

IMPORTANT LEGAL STUFF

While reasonable attempts have been made to ensure the accuracy of the information provided in this publication, the author does not assume any responsibility for errors, omissions or contrary interpretation of this information and any damages or costs incurred by that.

This book is not intended for use as a source of legal, business, accounting or financial advice. All readers are advised to seek the services of competent professionals in legal, business, accounting and finance fields.

While examples of past results may be used occasionally in this work, they are intended to be for purposes of example only. No representation is made or implied that the reader will do as well by using any of the techniques mentioned in this book.

The contents of this book are based solely on the personal experiences of the author. The author does not assume any responsibility or liability whatsoever for what you choose to do with this information. Use your own judgment.

Any perceived slight of specific people or organizations, and any resemblance to characters living, dead or otherwise, real or fictitious, is purely unintentional. You are encouraged to print this book for easy reading. However, you use this information at your own risk.

CHAPTER ONE

DEFINITION OF FREELANCE

"I didn't want an unsatisfying career. And I didn't want to commit to one place- either one company or one location. I wanted to make my own decisions." Rocco Baldasarre

The word "freelance" dates back to the medieval period where they had two different types of knights; the ones who worked exclusively for a particular king and those not attached to any king or lord. The knights who were not attached to a particular king worked as a mercenary for anyone who could paid them and were referred to as freelancers.

Basically, freelance describes a position which entails earning money by being hired to work on different jobs for short periods of time rather than by having a permanent job with one employer.

A freelancer is a self-employed person working in a profession or trade in which full-time employment is also common. A freelancer is a term normally used for a person who is self-employed and is not necessarily committed to a particular employer full term. Freelance workers are sometimes represented by a company that hire freelance labor to clients while others work independently. Freelance practice varies greatly among its practitioners. Some require clients to sign written contracts, while others may perform work based on verbal agreements.

One of the biggest misconception about freelancing is that freelancers are called that because they work for free or for peanuts. Freelancing is different from volunteering where people offer their skills for free or at low rates because they believe in the cause they are volunteering for or want to gain experience in a field they are interested in. As freelancers gain more experience in their field of specialization, they can command higher rates for their work. There is also a misconception that freelancers will just sit at home and have different jobs come to them when in reality freelancers have to put themselves out there to get jobs.

We are no longer in the medieval period where mainly knights were referred to as freelancers. We are in the

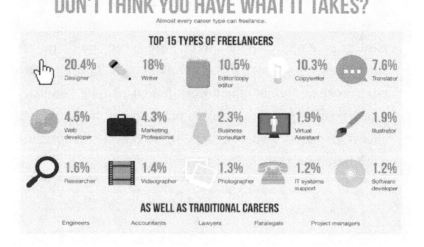

DON'T THINK YOU HAVE WHAT IT TAKES?
Almost every career type can freelance.

TOP 15 TYPES OF FREELANCERS

20.4% Designer	18% Writer	10.5% Editor/copy editor	10.3% Copywriter	7.6% Translator
4.5% Web developer	4.3% Marketing Professional	2.3% Business consultant	1.9% Virtual Assistant	1.9% Illustrator
1.6% Researcher	1.4% Videographer	1.3% Photographer	1.2% IT systems support	1.2% Software developer

AS WELL AS TRADITIONAL CAREERS

| Engineers | Accountants | Lawyers | Paralegals | Project managers |

twenty first century, a time that appreciates freelancers in hundreds of different jobs.

Sure, you have probably heard of freelance photographers too, you may have even met one or two in your life, but what about freelance software designers, freelance medical billing specialists, or even freelance scientific researchers? So, you really don't need to feel like you are skill less if you are considering freelancing as an employment path. In the list below, there is a broad spectrum of the different skills people need. Peradventure, your exact skill or specialization is not in the list, you can always learn one that is close to your initial feed or one that catches your fancy. To be candid, it is not difficult to learn majority of these freelance skills with Google and YouTube available. I know of someone who learned how to play the guitar reasonably well through learning on YouTube and if you set your mind on learning or improving any of the skills you want to freelance with, you can make something meaningful out of it.

Freelancing cuts across different fields, professions and industries which include:
- Administrative Assistance
- Advertising Consultant
- Animation
- Architecture

- Audio Production
- Bumper Sticker Design
- Business / Venture Funding
- Business Planning
- Business Writing
- Career Counselling

"Don't freelance to make living- freelance to make a life. Money is important- but when you hit ruts, work 16-hour days and get that tough feedback, it's going to be something else that motivates you. You need to remember why you started and keep it in

- Catering
- Computer Networking
- Computer Programming
- Computer Technician
- Computer Training
- Copywriting
- Creative Writing – Children's Books, screenwriting, poetry e.t.c
- Customer Service
- Dog Training
- Dog Walking

- Drawing – Caricatures
- E-commerce
- Editing
- Employee Recruitment – Employment Agency
- Engineering – Civil, electrical, mechanical e.t.c
- Event Planning
- Event Promotion
- Fashion Design
- Financial Planning
- Fine Arts.
- Home Cleaning
- House Painter
- Image Management
- Interior Design
- Landscape design

FREELANCE AT A GLANCE

The popularity of mobile devices combined with the explosive growth of apps and cloud-based computing are making it easier than ever before for people to take their expertise out of the office and set off on their own. Whether they do it for the flexibility or the independence, freelancers are fast becoming the new face of the global workforce.

BACKGROUND OF A FREELANCER [1]

> Most Freelancers are Men

76.6%   23.4%

> Average Age of the Full-Time Freelancer:

32
YEARS OLD

> Where Do They Live?

More Than Half in North America

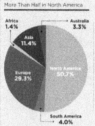

Africa 1.4%
Australia 3.3%
Asia 11.4%
Europe 29.3%
North America 50.7%
South America 4.0%

Attracted to the City

Rural (Less than 10,000) 7.5%
Town (10,000 - 100,000) 22.6%
Major City (1M +) 38.6%
Established City (100,000 - 1M) 31.4%

> Where Do They Get the Bulk of Their Training?

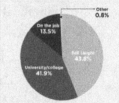

Other 0.8%
On the job 13.5%
Self taught 43.8%
University/college 41.9%

CLOCKING IN [2]

> Full Time or Part Time?

Full-time 49.7%
Part-time for additional income 36.6%
Part-time to transition to full time 13.6%

> Majority Work the Same or Fewer Hours

Compared to their previous full-time employment, most work either the same or fewer hours every week.

- 25.8% work more as a freelancer than previously
- 49.7% work the same or less than previously
- 24.5% never worked as a full-time employee in their industry

> South American Freelancers Work the Most

Among full-time freelancers worldwide, how many hours on average do they work per week?

NORTH AMERICA 39
EUROPE 41.2
ASIA 39.5
SOUTH AMERICA 49
AFRICA 38
AUSTRALIA 37.3

GETTING THEIR NAME OUT [3]

The majority of participants in the 2010 Global Freelancers Survey found jobs through referrals and the Internet rather than cold calling.

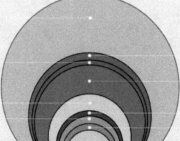

Referrals
Social networking sites 14.4%
Personal or professional blog
Cold calling 4.1%

Portfolio web sites 16.2%
Online job boards/sites 13.2%
Advertising (web, print, etc.) 4.8%
Other 3.2%

TYPES OF FREELANCING

1) Independent Contractors

This group accounts for the biggest amount of independent workers out there and they are probably what you have in mind when you think of the term freelancer. This category of workers freelances on a full time basis- they are hired on a project-to-project basis. You need to ensure that you perform your jobs well and be recognized as an expert in your field. Word of mouth is everything and you don't want people circulating bad reviews about working with you. Professional freelancers tend to work very hard as they are fully aware that their next project depends on the success of the one they are currently engaged in.

2) Night Workers

As the name explains, night workers are those who after their traditional 9 to 5 job, work on a side projects (normally at night) from time to time. These individuals do a little of both and must manage the two; full-time job, project-based work here and there. Some do this to make ends meet, or to have an extra source of income or to save up to start their own business.

3) Diversified Workers

While night workers tend to reserve their freelancing efforts to the night, diversified workers do a little bit of everything throughout the day. For example, a "typical" diversified worker will have one or more traditional, part-time job let's say, and also do some web-design freelancing on the weekend or on their spare time for example.

4) Temporary Workers

They are freelancers hired on a temporary basis, normally full-time, to work for a certain organization; independent consultants being the most obvious example in this category. The number of temporary workers is growing rapidly and offers variety to those who crave it.

5) Freelance Business Owners

This category of people are referred to as business owners because they have made a business out of freelancing rather than it being just a job. Freelancers in this category hire other people as freelancers too to handle some freelance jobs for them from time to time. Overtime, once a person is established as a freelancer, they tend to get more jobs than they can handle so they get other people who can handle it while keeping a percentage of the payment. Some people do not even get established as a freelancer but position themselves to get more jobs than any person can handle in a specific period of time while recruiting other people to the team.

CHAPTER TWO

FREELANCE STATISTICS

"The supreme accomplishment is to blur the line between work and play". -Arnold J. Toynbee

US Freelance Statistics

The Freelancers Union "53 million" report contains data results of the most comprehensive survey of the U.S. independent workforce in nearly a decade. Here are a few of the main stats from the report:

- There are 53 million people doing freelance work in the US – 34% of the national workforce.
- People who freelance contribute an estimated $715 billion in freelance earnings to the economy.
- Twice as many freelancers have seen an increase in demand in the past year as have seen a decrease – 32% experienced an increase versus 15% who have seen a decrease.
- 80% of non-freelancers say they would be willing to do work outside their primary job to make more money.

European Freelance Statistics

According to a report called "Future Working: The Rise of Europe's Independent Professionals", the European freelance economy looks like the following:

- Freelance numbers have increased by 45% from just under 6.2 million to 8.9 mil-lion in 2013, making them the fastest growing group in the EU labor market.
- Spain and Slovakia have both have 13% rates of self-employment
- Italy has a 21% rate of self-employment

UK Freelance Statistics

In the UK, the Professional Contractors Group estimates that:

- There are 1.4 million British freelancers working across all sectors.
- This has grown 14% in the past decade.
- The flexibility offered by Britain's freelancers is worth £21 billion to the UK economy in added value.

- 78% of the UK public think that freelancing and flexible working help promote a good work life balance.
- 72% think freelancing has a positive effect on family life.
- In 2013, the number of businesses hiring freelancers online increased 46%
- Payments to freelancers increased 37% year on year
- The average hourly rate for UK freelancers increased 6.7% in 2013
- IT & Programming (at 41% of all hires); Design & Multimedia (24%) and Writing & Translation (18%) make up the majority of freelance jobs online

CHAPTER THREE

IS FREELANCING FOR YOU?

"Destiny is no matter of chance. It is a matter of choice. It is not a thing to be waited for, it is a thing to be achieved."-Williams Jennings Bryan

Freelancing has been largely referred to by a lot of people as the 21st century way of making a living. In times past, it used to be seen as a field only journalists, actors, media persons and writers play in but now, it extends beyond those fields. More and more people are realizing that they can make far more money working for themselves as freelancers than they ever could solely from working under the wing of their previous employer. And as such, there are more people considering that job path in building their careers in the different available fields.

Chances are that at some point or another we have all wanted to go out on our own – away from our current jobs – and start a new career path as a freelancer in our field of specialization.

But why don't you? What holds you back from

going out and doing what it is that you want to do with our lives? Why do you allow ourselves to be tied to your employer as if some invisible shackles enslave you?

So, it sounds pretty good doesn't it? You work in some field for quite a few years, get a lot of practical experience in your chosen area of employment and then gradually make the switch from working the nine to five to becoming your own boss as a freelancer. Or you are just fresh out of the university or just finished learning a skill and decide to go straight into freelancing.

Stop for a moment, what types of skills do you need in order to finally break free from the nine to five shifts and start out on our own as a freelancer? You should ask yourself all of these questions before you even think about quitting your current occupation in pursuit of a freelance job. Each and every year, far too many people believe that they can simply quit their jobs and pursue a career as a freelancer in whatever their specific field may be – and far too many of them fail, only to go crawling back to their previous employer in hopes that he will give the destitute freelancer his former job back.

This unfortunate circumstance happens for one reason and one reason alone – the person who wanted to branch out on his own as a freelancer had no idea what to expect. People told him that he could be free, have as many days off as he wanted and retain all of the profits from his work. But nobody ever told him that he may have to work long and hard to meet deadlines, manage his finances himself, and compete with thousands of others for the same clients.

Before you begin any ventures into the world of freelancing, you should know that it is not all fun and games – a lot of serious thought must go into your actions if you are to be successful.

But is it really as easy as it sounds to become a freelancer and actually make a living doing work on a freelance basis? You also must keep in mind that there are quite a few freelancers out there who work full time or have some regular, steady income job, while juggling freelance work part time. This is not because they make a ton of money and only have to work a couple of days per week but because they actually have had some trouble finding work in the past and need a much more solid career option in order to make sure that they do not find themselves facing bankruptcy.

However, such a scenario does not have to happen to you if you are willing to do whatever it takes to become a freelancer. Your career switch may not happen overnight – but eventually you will become highly successful at what you do.

The big question here to answer is if freelancing is right for you. To start with, when you think of freelancing, what is the first thing that comes to your mind? It is easy to see someone who has the same skills as you freelance, making cool cash, with the latest gadgets and want to start doing the same thing he does. What happens when you don't get the same results as your friend gets, and you start to struggle? Does it mean freelancing is over rated? Therefore, you need to have a picture of what freelance will look like for you and not try to project someone's else results as your target.

However, if you do not take out time to understand what freelancing can look like overtime, you might make temporary success and not have anything to show for it in the long run. So, before you answer the above question I asked, take your time to ask freelancers around you or research a little on freelancing online and with the tips and practicable points given in this book, create a strategic plan for your freelance business.

Taking the Freelance Path

I learned through trial and error that the freedom of freelancing also comes with its own challenges. And to succeed, one has to be intentional, dedicated and put in the effort.

On the overall, freelancing might give you more choices on how you use your skills, but it is also a move from having just one boss to having many bosses. Every client whose project you are handling becomes your boss and you can be called at any time when the slightest thing goes wrong. And it is simply because freelancing is different from consulting; if you build a website for a client and it later develops a problem or can't perform a certain task that you should have covered when you built it, then you will probably have to work on the website again- especially if that function was stated in the project brief. When something breaks, you fix it, and when deadlines are looming, you're alone in the office finishing up.

Before you decide to move to freelancing, take a significant look at your core self, your situation in life, and your life-goals. It might be time for a change but consider these questions and factors before you take on freelancing fully.

1. The first step in making that jump from office work to freelance is to decide whether or not you have what it takes to become a freelancer. We all want to be our own boss, call the shots, make independent decisions and be fully in charge of projects. But do we all have the drive and dedication that it takes to be successful without the watchful eye of supervisors? Sadly, we don't. This is not bad as no one is born perfect. Albeit, sitting down to access your strength will give you foresight in measuring your

performance and point you in the direction of what needs to be improved on your profile.

2. Do you have a large enough skill set to make you stand out amongst the hordes of different people all seeking the same work as you? For instance, the fact that you are an excellent graphics designer doesn't stop other graphic designers out there from being equally as good or better.

> "The life of the professional writer- like that of any freelance, whether she be a plumber or a podiatrist- predicated on willpower. Without it there simply wouldn't be any remuneration, period."- Will Self

Therefore, you have to sit down and think about what makes you so special in the world of freelancers. What will be the cutting edge for you? Why should someone pay for your services over the services of other people out there.

3. Do you have the time management skills necessary to run your own freelancing operation and meet all of the deadlines set upon you by your clients? If you naturally have problems meeting deadlines, don't overlook it as something that will automatically take care of itself once you start getting freelance gigs. It doesn't work like that! What you should rather do is to look at sample projects

that you will like to work on, the number of days given and time yourself to work on it. Some freelancers delude themselves by saying they would go for projects with longer duration. What happens when you have a 5000-word writing project to deliver within 10 days and you submit on the 9th day and the client tells you, they don't like the angle or perspective you wrote the work from? How will you meet up within a day? Technically, you delivered on time but since the client is not satisfied, it means your job is not yet done. And if you do not meet up their requirement within the extra 1 day left, you may lose a client or get a not so good review.

4. Do you need a consistent income?

There are times in life when a steady income is a must. Paying child support? Have the kids in private school? College? How about some extra debt you were hoping to pay off? If you have inflexible demands on your income, it may be necessary to stick with your current job a little longer. Here is where you have to be honest with yourself. Don't just go shouting about how successful people take risks when you have family to support. It's possible to make more money freelancing, but it can come in at unpredictable times. The stress that can erupt from waiting on a check can ruin the freelance experience and put serious pressure on the relationships around you. Imagine you are working on another job, and a crucial problem crops up with your personal life, and the last job hasn't sent in the pay check? How do you concentrate on the freelance job you have at hand with such pressure? If you push it off to look for a way round the financial problem, when you resolve it, you will have to get another gig whilst other bills will be waiting.

5. Do you have insurance needs?

If you haven't discovered this yet, insurance is expensive. For instance, when you were in paid employment, you could get a car on mortgage, hire purchase, take loans and all that and maybe your company even provided full or partial health insurance coverage. But now that you are heading out on your own, this would be an expense you will need to compensate for. If you have health issues or a young growing family, it may be better to stay with your current job till your savings can handle your family, food, medical bills and other expenses for maybe a year. The added stress of trying to pay medical expenses can overburden a new freelancing career.

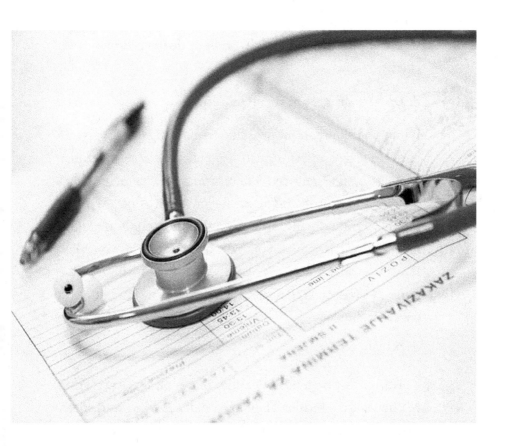

6. Are you too soft-hearted to be firm with clients?

I had a friend who hated contracting. He liked the work, but couldn't stand up to clients, struggled to set limits and wasn't firm about payment. He found himself continuing to make changes beyond the original scope and sometimes was unable to take back control of the project. Eventually, he had to quit contracting all together and found a job where he could use his skills without dealing directly with clients.

7. Do you struggle to be organized?

Being poorly organized will ruin freelancing fast. Everyone ends up angry and frustrated. Clients feel cheated because projects aren't delivered when promised. Payments don't come in because invoices never went out. Without organization, you end up working all the time to make up for the distractions that you have allowed crowd your day. If you're someone who doesn't want to deal with the fine details of a project, then find a job that fits that, but don't try to freelance.

8. Do you dislike dealing with clients?

This isn't just being soft-hearted; this is all the way. Truth is, clients are a hassle. They need hand holding and speak a language all their own. They have wants. They have needs. If all you want to do is create, then freelancing isn't for you. A business can't survive without customers — and if you're a business of one, no one else is there to manage them.

9. Do you actually want to run a business?

Take it or leave it, freelancing is a business and running a business comes with its own challenges. There's a lot to remember, a lot to organize, and a lot of responsibilities beyond creating the product. You can find help (accountants, billing software, etc.), but you will still have work on your end. Nothing can ruin a future faster than running a business poorly.

Legal issues can occur- even with clients. Poorly handled taxes can lead to audits and large bills. If you're not willing to take it seriously, walk away and find a job working for someone else.

10. Do you struggle to save money or manage finances?

One of the biggest struggles in the move to freelancing is income flow. There are times when clients are beating down your door and other times when everyone is off on vacation. Work comes and goes. You will have months where you might pull in substantial revenue as you've closed out a big project and other months where all your time went into business development and project management.

If you are someone who just can't save for the lean times, freelancing is going to be a consistent strain. Sure, some months you will have money to burn, but the next month you might have to call friends or take soft loans. Seriously, this happens a lot and can destroy your freelance career before it.

11. Is your community supportive?

Freelancing is stressful. From time to time, there will be constant pressure to finish the current project while at the same time establishing the next. Some days you work all the hours you can keep your eyes open knowing tomorrow will be exactly the same. It is a lot to take on and a solid support system is a strong pillar to hold you together through the days when all you do is wake, work, sleep, work. If stress is also coming from the people around you, it can feel like drowning. Balancing work, clients, and family is going to be hard enough. If your community isn't willing to be flexible, willing to be understanding, and willing to work with you, you could lose both them and your business.

I wouldn't advise you to go into freelancing if after reading these things you feel like you can't make the changes necessary to be sterling in your field, or if you have even the slightest doubt in your mind. The truth is not every employment path fits everyone and making money or building wealth doesn't come through freelancing or entrepreneurship alone.

Now that you have thought it over and you are absolutely sure that freelancing is right for you, it is time to set foot into your new career path and start looking for some work.

Whatever you do, do not quit your current job right now, as you will not have a livable source of income for at least a few months while you search for well-paying projects. Quitting your job will come in due time, but only after you have managed to net a few illustrious contracts first.

> *"Excellence is never an accident. It is always the result of high intention, sincere effort, and intelligent execution; it represents the wise choice of many alternatives- choice, not chance, determines your destiny." Aristotle*

Wi   our
nev   our
computer, pull open your web browser of choice, head over to one of the top three search engines, and look for work. Before jumping into your freelancing business with

both feet, you need to start off on the freelance path slowly before you can really start raking in the cash. If you have a job or a regular job offer, then don't quit your job just yet! Instead, you need to begin your hunt for freelance work in your area of expertise on the internet and see what you can come up with.

Some skills, such as the ability to write coherently or do software design for clients of all types, are highly marketable and you should really have no difficulty whatsoever finding a goldmine of work. On the other hand, if you are only able to do tasks that are not as easily marketable on a freelance basis, you will have much more difficulty finding work for your freelance operation. Essentially, I am simply saying that you should test out the waters if you can rather than leaving a steady income job and jumping into freelancing without surveying its terrain.

Currently some of the most popular fields for freelancing include writing, editing, photography, web and graphic design, software design, and architecture or drafting.

Once you have settled on a field that you want to freelance in, you will need to start finding your first clients. Whatever you do, do not start your hunt with any of the clients that you may have dealt with in your current job. There are all kinds of laws against this practice and it may get you into serious trouble if you are caught. You should rather search for new clients, then after a while of working with new clients, you may now reach out to clients you worked with in your former job.

If you are still in a full-time job, when you find you have some free time, all you have to do is search around on websites to find the freelance positions that sound good to you.

Another thing to note is that, when you just start out as a freelancer, you will probably have to take a few jobs that do not pay very well at all. That's fine because these jobs help you build your skill set. Your skill and experience might come in handy if you are applying for another job, but it doesn't count much with freelancing. The freelance work environment is different, so clients will want to see that you have had some experience delivering jobs remotely without having a supervisor hovering around or your colleagues to put heads together with you.

You shouldn't feel discouraged when you are seemingly getting the low paying jobs because they will help you learn how to effectively manage your time, speed up your workflow, and even help you get more used to using a computer and the internet to search for answers to any questions that may pop up while you are doing work for your client. The low paying jobs will probably last for a while, until you have assembled a massive list of satisfied clients. So, don't go too high on your price for a start as you will have to primarily compete with all of the other freelancers in your field entirely on how low your rates and fees are.

Eventually though you will graduate into higher and higher paying jobs until you will find that you have practically doubled your current income with income from freelancing. At this point you should feel confident enough to possibly start thinking about reducing the

> *"In the space between yes and no, there's a lifetime. It's the difference between the path you walk and the one you leave behind; it's the gap between who you thought you could be and who you really are; it's the legroom for the lies you'll tell yourself in the future."- Jodi Picoult*

number of hours you work at your current job to part time status or even quitting your job all together and make your fortunes solely through freelancing in your selected field.

Other Tips

- **Create and curate samples of your work.**

How else can you show prospective clients that you can write, design or create software? People need to see to believe. This is important because as you start getting small gigs, you tend to push off organizing your work and when a client asks you for a sample, you end up spending 2 or more days before getting back to them because you had to take time out to organize content and make it presentable. And that is bad for growing your freelancing business. You don't want to start by shooting yourself in the leg. So, organize your work into folders, classify them, highlight areas that need to be highlighted so that when clients call for your work they can measure your skills and what you are capable of delivering. Better still, you can upload them on Google Docs or Google Drive with a shareable link.

- **Target Your Portfolio**

Whatever type of portfolio you choose to create, be sure that it is targeted to the audience you are trying to attract, as there is no sense in including work you did as a software programmer if you are looking for work as a freelance photographer for example.

- **Host your sample somewhere.**

Now, you are just starting out so you may not have enough cash to splurge on a fancy website but there are a few places you can go to like Contently to host your portfolio. It is important that people can see your works stationed somewhere online, even before they have to ask you.

- **Be reachable**

It doesn't hurt to have so many ways for people to contact you. Let people know you are reachable and accessible. Don't just put an e-mail. If you can, put your other social media handles (especially LinkedIn) and have one social media platform where you constantly interact and engage with other people on topics related to your skills. That way people know there is some sort of credibility to working with you.

- **Print business cards**

Now, it looks like it is getting more expensive to set up a freelance business or side hustle, right? Which is why I said earlier not to just jump out of your job or decline a steady income job offer until you comfortably have a grasp of the freelancing terrain.

All the same, a business card adds a professional touch to your freelance career. It is a little more reassuring when you speak to someone about your freelance skill and give them a well-designed business card. People will see you more as someone devoted to building that skill and one who is very good at it because you are going all out as opposed to some other freelancers who only have verbal branding of their skill.

- **Attend industry events**

If you are keen on building your freelance skills, you can't sit down in the house and not connect with people who do something similar to what you do. Go out there and attend events, seminars and the likes. Take pictures, post them on your social media handles, tag other professionals you met at the event. That way you are building a cycle. When people are searching for persons with your skills to work with or people are searching for you and they see you with other professionals, they know you are fully in the game. Do not forget to hand out your card and collect the card of other professionals too.

Top drivers and barriers to freelancing

DRIVERS

☑ Freedom

☑ Flexibility

☑ Earning extra money

BARRIERS

☒ Income predictability

☒ Finding work

☒ Benefits

- **Develop a business mindset**

As much as freelancing sounds like a free and smooth ride, I can assure you that if you do not approach it like a business, it might not amount to something substantial or create financial independence. Remember that it is from your freelance career that you will build a rich pension fund, health insurance, money-making investments, take vacations and other things.

My candid piece of advice will be for you to start reading about successful business men, how big businesses were built, how the world's most profitable companies are run- especially if you never liked business from the scratch. Running a successful freelance career is akin to running a successful business and the most innovative, evolving businesses are the ones who stay on the scene longer.

CHAPTER FOUR

HOW TO START FREELANCING

"You can think of freelancing as volatile and risky, or as flexible and opportunity-rich. Doesn't having multiple sources of income and multiple moneymaking skills sound less risky than putting all your eggs in one employer's basket? Freelancing lets you shift gears when the world does." Sara Horowitz

Make an Inventory of Your Skills

If you are considering freelancing, you should choose an area that allows you to make use of your skills well. Whether you're looking for a new career or just starting out in one, it's always a good idea to keep an up-to-date inventory of your job skills or what service you are capable of rendering people for money. Naturally, we all have a tendency to get so caught up in the day-to-day activities and responsibilities that sometimes, we may not realize that we have certain skills we aren't using. Likewise, some people pick up new skills as part of their daily jobs, without even being conscious of it.

Taking a few minutes to assess your skills can be helpful when transitioning to freelance. While most people tend to know their own strengths and weaknesses and have a standard response when asked what their skills are, they probably aren't giving themselves enough credit. Just as you have to update your resume with each job you have had, you also need to regularly update the list (even if it's just a mental list) of your skills.

Our knowledge, skills and experience are constantly evolving, and even if you haven't changed jobs in a while, there are bound to be new tasks you have performed, new software you have been exposed to, or new issues you have had to address. Think about your recent experiences and make a list of anything new that you can identify. In addition, think about which of these responsibilities and tasks you have particularly enjoyed. This can help you identify new areas of interest that could lead to you pursuing different types of freelance projects.

How do you do this? You need to make an inventory of your freelancing skills by making a list of all your skills. Think of skills you picked up while you were employed-if you had a paid employment before. Think of things you have formally studied or trained for. And other skills within or outside your field that you learned on your own. Write until you can't think of anything more. And then ask your friends and family what they think you can do (again, not what you're good at but what you can already do). Stop only when you're sure you've exhausted all the possibilities. After completing your list, the next thing to do is to analyze your skills.

- which skills are you really good at?
- which skills do you enjoy doing most?
- which skills are in high demand?

And then, armed with the knowledge of what types of jobs would be good matches for both your skills and your personality attributes, you can start searching for the perfect job.

Chances are that when you start out down the road of a freelancer in any field you will find that you can only get small time, low pay contracts and projects that really do not require much skill at all. This is because you are new and relatively unknown to the freelance community. As time passes though, and you get client after client, more and more people will start to know who you are and the kind of work you will do. You can then net the higher paying projects that will allow you to really start supplementing your income greatly.

Eventually you may even find that some potential clients may start coming to you with their work, hearing how much you can accomplish or how good you are at meeting deadlines from the people who hired you previously.

Albeit, as an up and coming freelancer, the first thing you must do when looking for clients is to get your name out there. Let people know who you are, what you do, how well you do it, and what you can do for them. Potential clients love a freelancer who is willing to get the job done right the first time on a timely manner, and if you have no prior experience, you may have trouble getting high paying customers to trust you right off the bat.

However, if you start with a few low paying jobs, you will quickly find that you can advance through the ranks very rapidly and soon be able to net all of the projects that will allow you to keep your freelance business self-sufficient.

And like I mentioned in the previous chapter, as a first-time freelancer it is recommended that you create a mass of different items that can show off the kind of work you do. You can either include this portfolio as an email attachment when you apply for positions offered to you by clients, or if you have some web design skills you can create a personal portfolio website that outlines all of the specific projects that you have worked on over the years for various clients.

Use specific keywords that can describe what you want to do with your freelancing skills and sooner or later you will wind up with a massive database of different websites that cater to the freelance community in your specific field. It is highly important that you are this detailed. After all, if you are a freelance writer why would you look for work at the software programming freelance directories? Once you have constructed a list of the top websites in your field where you think you will be able to find clients, visit the sites daily (or subscribe to their RSS feeds) to find projects that would not only be interesting to you but will also pay the bills.

Note that you should only include projects that you have all of the rights to, as if someone thinks that you may have stolen pieces of your portfolio from others, the word may get out and you risk not being hired for freelance work by anyone – ever. Furthermore, only add items to your portfolio that make you look good in whatever particular field you are trying to find freelance work in. Don't put in all your work in your portfolio! Only the ones that are stellar and excellent.

Moreover, your competition from around the globe will be another major barrier in your pursuit to become a self-sufficient freelancer. People from all walks of life and from just about every country in the world will be competing for the same projects as you, so you had better be prepared to offer something that other people simply cannot compete with. For example, if you are a freelance writer or editor, the best way to compete is to explain to your clients that you are a native English speaker. Graphic and web designers as well as software programmers should take plenty of extra college courses to show how well they are educated in their craft.

Where to Look for Customers in Masses

So, you have finally decided to take that first big step in your career change towards the world of freelancing, but there is just one hitch – you have no idea where to find your first clients and customers.

A few years ago, you would have to act solely by means of local businesses and private residents of your community in hopes that someone, anyone you know could lead you to a potentially high paying client for your freelance work.

Writers always had it easier because there were hundreds of magazines and newspapers who always needed freelancers on a day to day basis – but if you were a web designer or a software programmer, chances are you were out of luck. But that was back before the internet wove its way into homes across the world.

Finding customers for your freelancing operation has never been easier thanks to the internet. People and companies looking for freelancer workers to help them with a project or two are all over the place and can help you get started in the freelance world if you are lucky enough to find a client that will work with you time and time again.

Furthermore, as a freelancer you can also use the internet to your advantage to advertise your services on various forums and other freelance web resources. In these situations, instead of you looking for some prospective clients, they look for you – allowing you to focus on whatever tasks and projects you are currently working on for others.

Now, when it comes to finding clients for your freelance business in masses, you need to focus your attention to the various forums and discussion boards that dot the web.

Google is a great way to search for different websites that are specific to your chosen freelance field, and if possible, you should avoid posting advertisements for your services in freelance forums that are not frequented by people who are looking for freelancers in your line of work. Posting out of section makes you look bad and could result in you being banned from various freelancing websites that may have proven helpful to you in the future as your business expands.

Because it is so important for you to find freelance websites that are focused to your particular field of operation, you need to decide on one or two services that you think you can find freelance work in and then go from there. If you choose one of the popular freelance jobs, such as writer, editor, photographer, web designer, or software programmer then you will have a much easier time finding work online because there are so many different freelance directories available to you.

As any kind of freelancer, one of the best places to start your search for customers from around the world is Craig's List. This is your one stop shop that can help you find work in your local metro area as well as in cities and countries from around the world. Most of the jobs offered at Craig's List allow you to work at home although you may have to visit the offices of some of the higher paying positions from time to time.

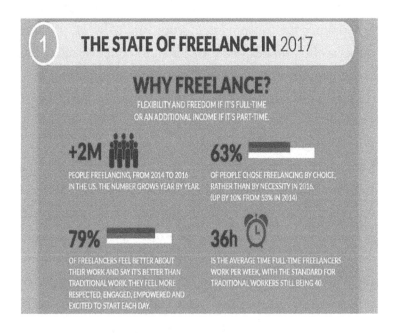

THE STATE OF FREELANCE IN 2017

WHY FREELANCE?
FLEXIBILITY AND FREEDOM IF IT'S FULL-TIME
OR AN ADDITIONAL INCOME IF IT'S PART-TIME.

+2M
PEOPLE FREELANCING, FROM 2014 TO 2016
IN THE US. THE NUMBER GROWS YEAR BY YEAR.

63%
OF PEOPLE CHOSE FREELANCING BY CHOICE,
RATHER THAN BY NECESSITY IN 2016.
(UP BY 10% FROM 53% IN 2014)

79%
OF FREELANCERS FEEL BETTER ABOUT
THEIR WORK AND SAY IT'S BETTER THAN
TRADITIONAL WORK. THEY FEEL MORE
RESPECTED, ENGAGED, EMPOWERED AND
EXCITED TO START EACH DAY.

36h
IS THE AVERAGE TIME FULL-TIME FREELANCERS
WORK PER WEEK, WITH THE STANDARD FOR
TRADITIONAL WORKERS STILL BEING 40.

Set Your Freelancing Goals

As a freelancer you need to set achievable goals, you must always set SMART goals.

What is a SMART goal? It is:

- Specific
- Measurable
- Attainable
- Realistic
- Time-bound

Specific. Your goal should be so specific that you can see it, feel it when it has actually happened. Literally, this means you can point to it or tell someone else about it. Rather than say I want to be rich from freelancing, you should probably say I want to make $12000 annually from freelancing.

Measurable. You should be able to measure or count your goal. When your goal is measurable, it's easy to see how much farther you have to go.

Like the goal set above, you can break it down to making a $1000 monthly from freelancing as that will amount to $12000 annually.

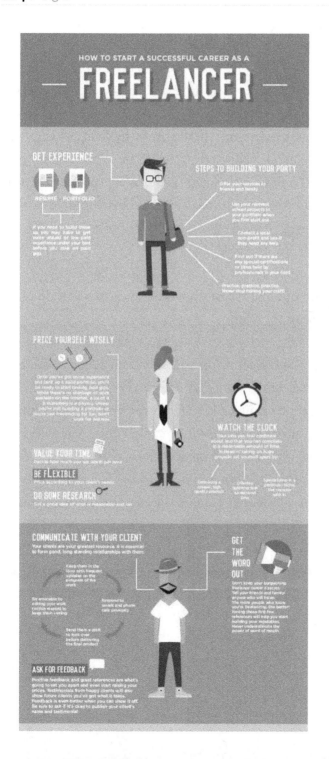

Attainable. Every personal development expert will tell you to dream big. Everyone says it, dream big, dream big! And dreaming big is so true and important but practical goal setters will tell you to dream big within your reach. Does this mean you should only look at what people around you has achieved? No. It means you should not set a $12000 annually revenue goal if your current skill set is not strong enough for whatever freelancing field you are considering. Rather you should improve your skill set before setting that goal else it would be mere wishing. Your goals should stretch you beyond your comfort zone, not beyond your ability and capability such that you do not set yourself up for failure.

Realistic. Set goals you can achieve in reality not just in your head. For instance, it will not be realistic for you to set a goal of earning $12000 in revenue when that amount is only paid to people with both skill and experience and you have only skill! Remember your client would want to ask for proof of your previous work. So, it would make more sense to garner experience earning lesser amounts in order to build your portfolio.

Time-bound. Your goal should have a time element. The goal of earning $12000 in a year has a time element attached to it so you know that by 1 year you are to take stock to see if you achieved that.

Check on Your Competitors

Rather than being intimidated by top freelancers and sulking about not being good enough, get around to knowing your competitors. That way you can learn about their skills, portfolios which will serve as cues for improving yourself too.

Here are a few ways to find them:

- **Google**
- **Twitter.** Go to search.twitter.com and type in your industry or service or even the name of a specific person.
- **Industry forums.** Keep your eyes open for service providers forum participants recommend.
- **Elance**

- **Your target clients.** Ask them whom they hire for specific services. They're usually responsive on Twitter.

Look at the professional websites of your competitors or check out their Linkedin profiles or their profiles on freelance websites or job sites for the following information:

- The kind of services they offer
- How much they charge
- Who their clients are or who they have worked with
- How they present and market themselves
- What their unique selling proposition is
- What your target clients want which your competitors don't address

The goal is not to do what your competitors are doing but to take a leaf from them in setting yourself up as a freelancer and to distinguish yourself from every other person freelancer out there.

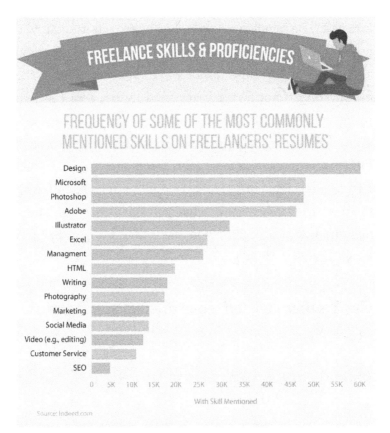

FREELANCE SKILLS & PROFICIENCIES

FREQUENCY OF SOME OF THE MOST COMMONLY
MENTIONED SKILLS ON FREELANCERS' RESUMES

Source: Indeed.com

Network to Find Clients

Networking is about building relationships. And through networking, it is easier and faster to find clients than through mainstream marketing. To get started on finding your ideal clients use Google to find suitable forums. Type into Google: "(niche or industry) forum." For example, if you're targeting software developer professionals, you would search for "software developer professionals' forum." The challenge with this approach is that you might not be eligible to join some of the forums. But you should get at least one forum where you can join. In the event, you do not find a specialized forum, you can join some general forums, look for threads where they talk about freelancing and pitch in. Another way to approach this is to network with those who are already in your target clients' circles that are accessible, build a relationship with them and let them know what you have to offer. These persons may never hire you but can refer you to your target clients.

Get Testimonials Of Your Freelancing Prowess

WHERE DO FREELANCERS FIND JOBS?

Almost half of freelancers find projects via online freelance marketplaces. The growing popularity of marketplaces has helped millions of freelancers build a worldwide client base.

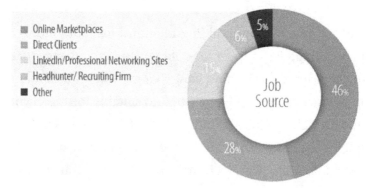

- Online Marketplaces
- Direct Clients
- LinkedIn/Professional Networking Sites
- Headhunter/ Recruiting Firm
- Other

Testimonials are important so your prospects know you're a reliable service provider ant not someone that will abandon them in the middle of an urgent job. If you are just starting out as a freelancer there are some alternatives to get testimonials when you don't have one client yet.

Contact your previous employers and bosses

You could approach your previous employers and bosses to give you a review. Make sure to get permission to use the feedback, as well as the person's full name, location (city and state will do), website URL, and photograph. When it comes to client testimonials or feedback, the more details you provide, the better. You'll want prospective clients to know that these are real people. As with references, your prospects should be able to trace these people and contact them, if necessary. And perhaps you have never worked before, you can approach former classmates or friends who are aware of your skill and can give a review that highlights that skill. Explain that you're going into freelancing and need feedback to include in your marketing materials.

Do free work in exchange for testimonials

This is a good strategy if you have absolutely no testimonials or have very few to begin with. You will find many people who are interested in this kind of bartering in the forums that you should be a member of. You could always say that you only want their honest feedback both positive and negative. Or, that you want their testimonial only if they are genuinely happy with your services. Otherwise, you welcome their suggestions for improving yourself.

A benefit of this strategy is that these "free clients" could become eventually regular paying clients. Or, they could refer paying clients to you later on.

Build Your Freelancing Portfolio

Many potential clients are not bothered about any qualifications you have, they simply want to see what you have done in the past and judge whether it is the right fit for them Therefore, if you are good at what you do and can demonstrate your skills through a quality portfolio and positive client testimonials, you have every chance of success. To work for high-paying clients, you need to demonstrate that you are *worth* big money by doing good work. So, don't be afraid to do *pro bono* work for the "right clients" when you are first starting out. Make sure they are clients who will utilise the service you offered them not just people seeking free services for multiple projects that they are not sure will scale through. The free work you do at this stage can ultimately be priceless when it clearly communicates your worth to future potential clients via an extensive portfolio and glowing testimonials. Also, offering your services at no cost is a gentle introduction into the world of freelancing where you do not feel the pressure of having to deliver a service of requisite value.

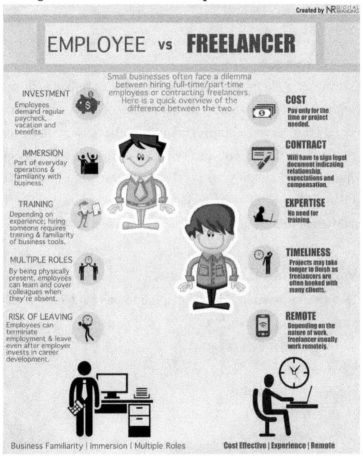

EMPLOYEE vs FREELANCER

Created by NR

Small businesses often face a dilemma between hiring full-time/part-time employees or contracting freelancers. Here is a quick overview of the difference between the two.

INVESTMENT
Employees demand regular paycheck, vacation and benefits.

IMMERSION
Part of everyday operations & familiarity with business.

TRAINING
Depending on experience; hiring someone requires training & familiarity of business tools.

MULTIPLE ROLES
By being physically present, employees can learn and cover colleagues when they're absent.

RISK OF LEAVING
Employees can terminate employment & leave even after employer invests in career development.

COST
Pay only for the time or project needed.

CONTRACT
Will have to sign legal document indicating relationship, expectations and compensation.

EXPERTISE
No need for training.

TIMELINESS
Projects may take longer to finish as freelancers are often booked with many clients.

REMOTE
Depending on the nature of work, freelancer usually work remotely.

Business Familiarity | Immersion | Multiple Roles   Cost Effective | Experience | Remote

Decide On Your Ideal Client

The first question you need to ask yourself is, "Who is my ideal client?" To answer this question, you need to figure out:

- who wants your services
- who is willing and able to pay what you want to charge

You want a client who wants your services rather than one who needs it but may not be aware of it. A client may need your services but not want it. In that case, you'll have to educate that client and work that much harder to get him or her to want your services. On the other hand, with clients who want your services, your only task will be to convince them that you're the best person for the job.

Who Is Your Target Client?

Determine as many specific qualities as you can about your target client, such as:

- gender
- age
- marital status
- residence
- occupation
- annual income
- industry
- life goals

- hobbies

Or think of specific people you know who fit into your idea of your target client. The next step is to find out what your target client wants. Getting to know your target client is now much easier than ever, thanks to the Internet. If you can identify 2-3 specific people online who fit the profile of your target client, your market research will get much easier. Here are some things you can do:

- Follow them on Twitter and listen to their Twitter stream.
- Read their blog. Comment and start interacting regularly.
- Subscribe to their newsletter.
- Be a fan of their Facebook page.

If you're feeling up to it, you might even request a quick Email interview. Ask three questions, tops, so choose your questions well. Even if you don't have specific people in mind, you should, at the very least, research the general industry you're interested in freelancing.

- Go to Google and look for the most relevant sites, blogs and forums in the industry.
- While you're in Google, set up your Google reader to send you daily Emails with the latest updates on the industry.
- Search for the industry term in Alltop.com.

- Use Tweet deck or Twitter search to see what people are tweeting about

As you're doing all this, take note of the problems people are stressing about. Do any of your skills address these problems? Also, be on the lookout for mention of service providers who seem to be doing well in your target clients' circles.

By now you should have a pretty good idea of what your target clients want. However, this is an ongoing exercise. You need to keep track of your target clients and the industry they are in. Set aside a few minutes every day or every week to visit the sites, blogs and forums you discovered.

What about forums you have to pay to join? If your budget allows it, join the best one. It'll be well worth it if the forum allows you to interact with your target clients. For now, keep that image of your target client in your mind. He or she will be the most important person in your freelancing business from now on.

CHAPTER FIVE

ESTABLISH AN ONLINE PRESCENCE

"Do your best work, deliver it before the deadline and exceed expectation" Kelly Abeen

If you are just starting your freelance career or fairly new to the social media and internet world, building your online presence can be time consuming and, at times, frustrating. Nonetheless, it is *very important.*

Building your online presence can be frustrating because it is not just something that happens overnight; and it is very important because your online presence is what allows people to find you, interact with you, and get to know, like and trust you.

An online presence can be described as the sum of all the identities you have created either personal or business driven or both, and the interactions those identities have established, and participated in, online.

Basically, your online presence has a very broad reach, and when built successfully it can spread brand awareness and gain you fans, followers, leads, customers and anything else you could ever want for your business.

How to start building your online presence

Not sure where to start with building your online presence? There is a lot that goes into building your online presence, from establishing your goals, to actually creating your different profiles and accounts, to building a website (your home base), all the way to figuring out the best ways to engage and interact across these different mediums. But it can be less time consuming and less frustrating if you know where to start.

One of the first main thing you should do is setting up your own professional website. Even if your target clients are offline businesses, you should still have a professional website- see it as a type of house or storage for your reputation. Besides, your prospective clients are sure to Google your name when they scope you out. What will they see when they do this? Hopefully, they'll find a website that's professional, easy to navigate or a profile well written with glowing reviews and portfolio briefs you have worked on which will convince them that you're the person to hire. Another reason you should have a professional website is because it will work for you, like a brochure, resume or business card that's available 24/7 – as long as your website is up and running, of course.

Other Strategies

1. Strategize

First and foremost, it's important that you understand what your business goals are – both short-term and long-term. As you start to build and grow your online presence, you should be constantly asking yourself how each of your online efforts are helping you take a step towards your business goals.

Write your goals down as related to building an online presence so you can easily refer back to them when you're measuring results, progress to make sure that what you are doing online is helping you take a step forward. Don't just build an online presence because everyone is doing it or because you are "supposed to", build it strategically and intentionally so that it can help your overall business goals.

2. Build a solid platform

Like I said earlier, start with your website which is your home base. Your website is your hub: a centralized place where people can go to learn more about what you have to offer, contact you, and interact and engage with your content.

Let your website offerings be clear. Make sure people can understand and grasp what freelance skills you offer. Easy-to-use navigation, an opt in giveaway, -so you can start building your email list- this could be 10% off their first contract especially if you have a per hour or per project rate. There should be a contact page, an about page, and some type of valuable content as required.

SEO is an important part in building your freelance game, from meta tags to title, description. Not an SEO expert? There are a ton of resources out there that can help you. Ask for help from those around you who have enough knowledge to help you get started. The Google Keyword tool is also a great resource if you want to start with at least finding out what keywords you want your website to rank for.

3. Keep optimizing and improving.

Do not ever get stuck in thinking that you can't put something out there until it's perfect – it is never going to be perfect. Just start, knowing that you will always be improving upon your content and what you have to offer. Continuously looking for ways to improve and optimize your site and your content post-launch is key to staying strong.

It is a continuous process- you are never there totally.

4. Provide consistent value

Whether it's via your website, an online community, or through your social media channels, you should always be looking to provide consistent value *first and foremost.* What content are you providing your audience?

It might be a blog, a podcast, videos or books; whatever form that content takes, make sure it's consistent and valuable. For the graphics person, you may talk about branding, using samples from your works.

Creating consistent and valuable content will help you gain credibility and authority in your industry or niche, which is important for your online growth and visibility.

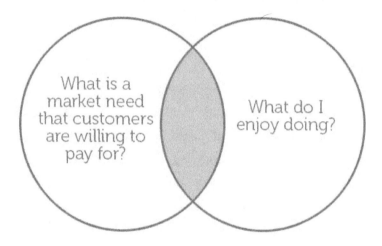

You could go further to analyze other people's works too. Ask yourself, what type of content or knowledge can you share with your community and followers that might not be your own content, but that will still be of value to them? A mix of 80 / 20 is a rule I like to follow: share other peoples' content 80% of the time, and your own content 20% of the time.

This will not only build trust with your followers as they will start to recognize that you are not just in it for yourself, it will also help you build relationships with others in your industry or niche (through sharing their content with your audience). It is also a great way to reach others' followers who might be interested in your content, too!

5. Be social

One of the greatest things about the Internet is that it allows you to be everywhere. Although, that doesn't translate to your spreading yourself thin. What I did while starting out was to take a platform at a time, build some results with it then try out other platforms. Try out the platforms out there then choose two or three social channels that work best for you. Preferably, start with two, establish some following and audience then add one more.

Really, being social doesn't mean you have to have a Facebook page, Twitter profile, Instagram handle, Google+ profile, Pinterest board, Snapchat, Quora blog, Reddit account, YouTube channel, LinkedIn profile and so on. But you should have at least two or three of these profiles set up that you regularly post and engage on. Consistency here is key. If you're not able to manage your social channels by posting regularly and being a part of the conversation, then it would be hard to increase your following.

Social media can be a great marketing tool to help you gain those initial fans and followers, and once you have those followers, it is left for you to reach out to them and engage with them.

6. Start building relationships

Something that is really important when you're trying to build your online presence is, of course, "being seen". If no one knows you, then presumably they won't be looking for you on your website, on Facebook, Twitter, LinkedIn and so on.

So what's the best way to draw people into your world? Find a group or online community that is made up of individuals who share the same interests or who run similar businesses in your industry or niche.

Then, build relationships with them through providing value and being an active member in the group. If you're just starting out, chances are these people are better connected than you are, and they might be able to help introduce you to others who are in your industry or niche. You should also find a group or community of individuals who fit the description of your audience, or ideal client because joining this type of community has the potential to give you priceless insights into what their biggest pain points are. Knowing this can help you pivot and create the exact content they want and need.

Again, always start by adding value for others first. If you are new to a group or community, it is important for you to not advertise yourself or your business. Once you start building strong relationships with others in the community, they'll naturally become interested in what it is you have going on, and you can start to share your content over time.

7. Track

You can start building your online presence today, but how do you know if it is working?

You'll know if you're tracking your progress. Every single week I look at the number of likes we have on Facebook, the number of Twitter followers we have, comments, posts that perform well, what people are asking, who shared which post and other insights like that. Google Analytics is also a great way to track your website traffic.

If you do not track these things, then you won't be able to recognize trends or identify why a large spike in traffic (or a decreased number of visitors) may have happened. It is important to test different things and figure out what's working best for you.

For example, guest posting which is a great way to get your name out there, build relationships with other freelancers in your niche, and show people the value you have to offer. It could result in increased traffic to your website, a strong backlink and a lot of social love, but only if you're tracking these things. Being able to track your online presence may not necessarily help you increase revenue immediately, but it will help you establish what is working for your business and what's not., improve visibility and ultimately get you clients.

Other Hacks
- Create Google Alerts or Talkwalker alerts for key brand, industry, client and competitive terms.

- Look into tools that allow you to create content funnels such as Survey Funnel, Spring Metricsor Get Smart Content
- Create Twitter Lists for clients, competitors and key media contacts.
- Create Feedly account and find twenty-five industry related blogs to follow
- Investigate social settings in your CRM and add Rapportive to your email.
- Investigate social tools such as TweetDeck, HootSuite or SproutSocial to help monitor mentions
- Add paid options like Radian6 or Trackur for deeper listening metrics

Summarily, your online presence has huge potential to get you and your business known through various online channels. But it takes time, and so you have to be patient. If you're able to start building a strong platform, create consistent and valuable content, establish a presence on social media, and build meaningful relationships online, then momentum will be on your side.

The way you interact and connect with people online can help expand your reach (brand awareness) while simultaneously growing the number of fans, followers, leads and customers your business has. You don't have to be everywhere online, but you do have to be somewhere online.

CHAPTER SIX

CLIENT COMUNICATION PROCESS

"The single biggest problem in communication is the illusion that it has taken place"- Peter Drucker

Communication is important no matter who you work with, but as a freelancer, good communication is key. The better you communicate with your client up front, the fewer revisions they are likely to ask for.

We all think communication is easy until we have clients, who give us a project and at the end of the project, it seems like we didn't get their specifications neither did they understand your promised output. Working with a "bad" client is even worse as it can add a ton of stress to your life and make you wary of future projects. And sure, there's likely to be a few genuinely bad clients out there who don't know what they want or are just plain rude. But the vast majority of freelance disagreements is related to miscommunication.

Ways to Effectively Communicate

1. Connect How You're Most Comfortable

Some clients just want to talk to me on the phone. And I oblige. But whenever I can, I like to connect via email which is because I am more comfortable that way, and it's easier for me to understand what the client wants when I read it rather than hear it. Figure out how you work best, and then connect that way.

2. Get It In Writing

Even if you prefer to conduct business over the phone (or via video chat), make sure you get it in writing. At the end of a phone conversation, send a summary email to confirm what you talked about, and what the client wants. Make sure the client replies in the affirmative (or with changes) before you start.

3. Keep It Professional

When you start with a freelance client, you need to keep the communication process professional. I do have some clients that I know well on a personal basis, and things are a little less formal with them. However, in many cases, when we're discussing new projects or negotiating pay, or dealing with business related issues, the communication becomes more professional.

4. Establish Expectations

One of the best ways to avoid or reduce conflict in your freelance project is to establish and manage expectations.

Clear communication is how you can accomplish this, of course, but a few actionable steps you can take include:

- Create a solid plan. The more information you have committed to pen and paper about a project, the more likely it is that you'll prevent the whole thing from falling off the rails.

- Use client questionnaires. You're going to want to ask potential clients as many questions as possible about what they want before you begin. This helps to reduce surprises along the way (for both of you), shorten project length, and reduce the number of revisions required. There are tons of examples online but I found two—one on Scribd and one on Tuts+—that seem especially apt here.

- Create a proposal and budget. Once you've run through all of your questions and come up with a vision for the project, write it down. This is your proposal. Make it as detailed as you can. Include all relevant deliverables and their respective dates.

- Develop a project scope. This is a part of your proposal and contract but I wanted to make sure I called it out by name here because it's so integral to project success. Set a limited number of revisions to help mitigate this as much as possible.

- Sign contracts. Both parties need to sign a contract. No question. You both need to agree to the terms laid out in your proposal and scope. You also need to agree on the budget. Having all of this down in writing with signatures attached will help to prevent confusion and disagreements later on.

5. Establish Deliverables

I mentioned deliverables when talking about contracts above, but they warrant their own section. It is often the case that the biggest stressors related to web development projects involve deliverables in some way, whether it's due dates or what the deliverables actually are.

These are things you need to pinpoint before you even get started on a project (or very shortly after beginning):

- What the main deliverable is: in this case, it's likely to be pretty clear. It's likely you'll be delivering a website.
- How many parts will make up the deliverable? It's always a good idea to break it down into logical parts. So, a website might be broken down into a site outline, a homepage design, a store design, etc. You can do it page by page, feature by feature, or whatever else makes sense for your given situation.
- When will you submit deliverables? Assign a due date to each of the parts above and make sure you leave enough time for revisions.

- How will you submit deliverables? Will you create a password-protected environment for clients to log in and view the progress on their project? Will you email mockups?
- How should the client provide feedback? Make sure your expectations are spelled out in terms of how you want to receive input from the client.

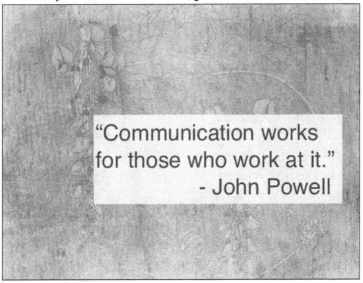

"Communication works for those who work at it."
- John Powell

6. Ask Questions

If there's something you're not clear on, don't be afraid to ask questions. You want to make sure that you know what the freelance client wants, and that you are clear on it. That's really important if you want to avoid endless revisions — or an outright rejection of the work you just put in. Clarify when the situation calls for clarification, and do it *before* you get to work, or move on to the next phase.

7. Provide Advice When Needed

If you see something that could be done differently or better, offer advice. Be tactful about it, and honest — especially if the client asks for your feedback. Your helpful feedback, advice can enhance the project, and make the client happier.

8. Be Specific

One of the biggest mistakes freelancers in general make is failing to ask the right questions. It is not your job to read the client's mind. It is their job to tell you what they want. Many freelancers approach a project as though they need to have the answer for everything right off the bat, but that's not necessary. Hearing the client out and determining what features they want is your best bet.

But if the client is having trouble articulating what they want, what do you do then? Ask specific questions.

Simply asking the client, "What do you want on your website?" isn't enough, however. You need to get specific. Here's a list of questions to have on hand if you're having trouble getting to the bottom of what a client wants:

- What do you want your site to accomplish?
- How do you plan on using the site to further your business goals?

- Do you have a company style guide?
- Are there examples of sites you'd like to mirror?

9. Don't Make Assumptions

About anything. Ever. You may think you know what the client wants but unless you want to risk having to start a project over again, clarify every detail before you sink any time into a site. If you've invested time in asking questions and creating a detailed contract, you should be good to go.

Another detail a lot of people forget when working with a new client. Is your contact person the one making the decisions at the company? Or do they answer to someone else? You need to know this because your contact might make a passing comment like, "This looks good," because it's their opinion. Then, a few days later you could get a message that says, "Well, actually, we want to move in a different direction." And unless you ask point blank sometimes, you might not know this important detail.

So, find out who has the power to make decisions client-side. Then adjust your expectations to meet this information. If there are several people who will have a final say in the site's design, come to an agreement about when they will let their opinions be known. Set clear deadlines for the client to provide feedback, too.

Finally, setting a clear revisions limit in your contract (as we discussed above) can help clients see that it's in their best interest to make sure all parties who want/need to be involved in the decision-making speak up in a timely manner.

Client Communication Templates

Creating templates will help you systematize communication with your clients.

What kind of templates do you need?

Your templates should include:

- Project proposal/bid/quotation
- Terms of agreement or a contract
- Submission of completed project
- Invoice
- Receipt
- Request for feedback

Your templates don't need to be fancy in terms of the layout. Use your business name and logo, if you have one. Otherwise, your name will suffice.

Basic Principles of Client Communication

When preparing your templates, keep these basic communication principles in mind:

- **Be professional.** You don't need to be stiff and formal, but don't use colloquial terms, either. Even if your prospect is a friend or acquaintance, make it clear in your communication that this is a commercial transaction.

- **Be extremely detailed, specific and clear**
  You can avoid a lot of misunderstanding by making sure that expectations are clearly spelled out. By this I mean, what the client can expect from you (such as outputs and deadlines), as well as what you expect from your client (for instance, prompt replies to your queries and timely payment).

- **Avoid Jargon**

> *"Take advantage of every opportunity to practice your communication skills so that when important occasions arise, you will have the gift, the style, the sharpness, the clarity, and the emotions to affect other people." Jim Rohn*

A client will find it difficult to make informed decisions if they don't understand what you are saying? While talking to other professionals in your field, you can easily use jargon, but you must make an effort to put things in simpler terms when speaking with clients. Sometimes, clients will agree to your approach on a project even when they don't really get what you are saying because they see you as the expert and might not want to question what you have said. However, imagine their surprise and the confusion when you submit the project, and it is not at all what they envisioned. They will still feel bad when they realize they agreed to something they didn't want. Take the time to explain and define terms they need to know to make decisions about how their project will come out when you are done.

- **Be positive**

Always be gracious in your communication. It never hurts to say "thank you" all the time. Even when you're demanding something from you client, you can state it in a positive way. One way to do this is to always state things in terms of how your client will benefit from fulfilling your request.

For instance, "I need your response by tomorrow, so I can submit the first draft on Tuesday."

- **Double-check and then check again for accuracy.** Before sending out anything to your client read and re-read and then read the piece again. Make sure everything is accurate: the client's name, company name, contact details, project details, deadlines, rates and other details.

- **Be a Better Listener**

  Sometimes, you can eliminate conflicts just by simply being a better listener. If you have asked the client a bunch of questions, you have plenty of information to work from. Go over your notes and see if you can distil what your client wants to a simple statement. Then, keep this statement in mind during all future interactions with the client too. If a conversation seems to contradict the information from your initial interviews, ask the client for clarification. Perhaps you've simply misunderstood. Or they have momentarily forgotten their main objectives. Regardless, listening ensures you and the client remain on the same page at all times and you continually meet each other's expectations.

- **Practice Client Interviews**

A lot of the success of moving forward with stress-free projects is to be a clear and concise communicator. You wouldn't always have the luxury of emails especially on some type of projects. If speaking is not your strength, it would be a good idea to practice with some of your colleagues. One of you can pretend to be the client on a fake project of your choosing. Then you can take turns role-playing. It is a great way to play out how a client interview might go and to see what kinds of questions elicit the most informative responses.

- **Don't Let the Client Wonder**

Going a few days between communications with a client is not strange, especially if you're really engrossed in a project. However, if your client calls you or emails you, try to respond the same day if you can. This shows you are attentive and makes the client feel like a priority. If the client gets antsy and has to check in with you to see how a project is coming along, you've waiting too long. Of course, some clients expect immediate results straightaway but for the most part, just keep them in the loop. You can make exceptions to non-business hours or on the weekends. Even if you work at 2 a.m., it is a good work line demarcation to not make a habit of responding to emails at that time. It will give off the impression that you are always available. Boundaries are a good thing.

> No matter what job you have in life, your success will be determined 5% by your academic credentials, 15% by your professional experiences, and 80% by your communication skills.

- **Stand Up for the Client's Best Interest**
  You should always listen to what the client has to say, and you should respect their input. However, sometimes a client will be wrong. The key is knowing when to let it go and when to stand your ground. If you run into a disagreement on an aspect of the project, take a step back and evaluate what the client is saying. Are they simply misinformed? If so, provide context and as much information as possible about why things need to

remain the same or whatever else fits the situation. However, if it is something minute or an issue of preference, it might be best to let it go.

CHAPTER SEVEN

PART TIME FREELANCING

"I am working full time on my job and part time on my fortune"- Jim Rohn

For those who do not want to take a big leap into full time freelancing yet, you could still survive part time freelancing while building some sort of structure for successful transitioning into full time freelancing.

Of all the side hustles you can do while keeping your day job, freelancing is one of the most feasible. At its core, you are essentially using your skills–the tasks and abilities you have already mastered–to take on contract work and augment your income. What's more, it's attractive for many reasons beyond just the money.

But, before getting started with your freelance business, you need to get very clear on why you want to freelance in the first place. Once you have your goals in mind, how you use your limited amount of time will greatly determine your level of success with freelancing.

1. **Have a Vision and Goal Board**

Yes. As a part time freelancer, you should have a vison and goal board for your freelance career, especially now that you still have another regular job. That way when you decide to go fulltime, it would be easier.

2. Build a portfolio

Start curating your previous projects into a place so that prospective clients can go through your works and see what you are capable of doing.

3. Set up financial processes

Set your prices, rates, get invoice templates, a reliable process of billing, freelance account to track funds, payment style (whether you want full or part payment before you embark on the project).

4. Marketing Style

Choose the marketing method that works best for you and begin to test them now to measure project traffic, which channels are more effective, what approach needs to be changed and all that.

"There are no safe choices. Only other choices" Libba Bray

5. Find a profitable niche

Your skill may cover a wide range of projects, but you need to pick a niche that is profitable and will work well for you. For instance, if you are a writer, you cannot excel in copy writing, content development, academic writing, business writing, technical writing at the same time. There should be one or two aspects of writing that you can do excellently in; that is the area you should focus your energy on and market. Just make sure it is a profitable niche. If you are good in a niche that isn't well patronized, you may do yourself good by learning a profitable niche while offering exclusive service in your niche.

6. Learn how to pitch

Often times, I find that people are shy when it comes to marketing or blowing their own trumpets but who else will do it for you? This is the perfect time to start out learning how to pitch your services and market yourself when you do not have anything to lose yet. The worst that will happen; they will say No, and you still have your job. So, what is there to lose?

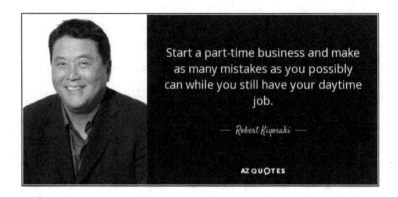

Here are the basics of pitching successfully:

- Make a strong entrance with an elevator pitch email that already provides immense value and shows you've done your homework.
- Sell your strengths.
- Anticipate and answer any questions that may come up.
- Lean on relevant work samples and past projects to demonstrate your expertise.
- Use a visually appealing layout for your proposal.

7. Don't Mix Your Regular Job Priorities With Freelance.

A lot of people make this mistake and end up being fired before getting their footing in freelance or leaving the company on a wrong note. Your day job is your source of reliable income, make it your No. 1 priority.

*Don't do anything to jeopardize your full-time employment, as you still need it to sustain you while you grow your freelance business on the side.

*Don't breach any contracts or agreements you signed with your employer.

*On no occasion should you do freelance work during company time.

*Avoid using company resources, computers, or online tools for your freelance work.

CHAPTER EIGHT

MARKETING YOUR FREELANCE BUSINESS

"I think a lot of attracting good clients is knowing who you want to work with and the type of work you want to do. Getting really specifc about your dream client helps to clarify things in your mind and allows you to filter out people who may not align with your core values"
Anonymous

Your marketing plan is how you intend to get in front of your target clients, how you intend to let them know you exist, offer the services they want and get them to hire you. Your marketing plan should have the following:
- Your freelancing goals and objectives
- An analysis of your target client.
- Marketing activities
- Schedule of implementation
- Monitoring and evaluation

Marketing Activities & Schedule
Under marketing activities, brainstorm how you can meet your target clients, or network with those who interact

with them regularly. Here are some examples of marketing activities:

- Publish a blog post weekly about a topic your target clients are interested in.
- Submit articles in article directories.
- Create a Twitter/Face book/LinkedIn account and network with prospective clients there.
- Join an online forum.
- Attend a live conference.
- Give away a white paper or special report.
- Join freelancing job boards and bidding sites.

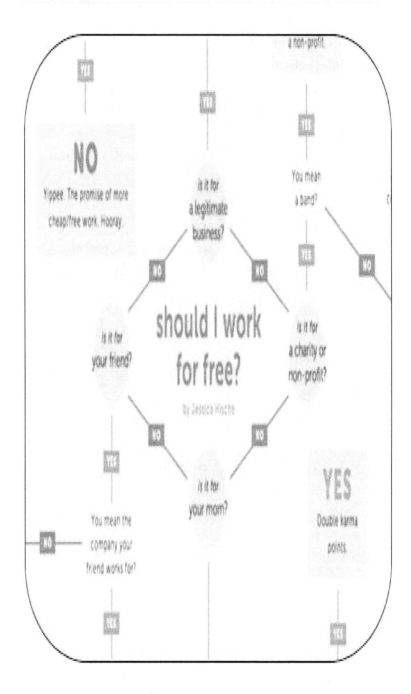

Until you get yourself fully booked, marketing is an ongoing activity. Even then, you'll still have to continue networking and marketing, although on a much lesser scale – just in case your current projects dry up or end.

Monitoring and Evaluation

"The best marketing doesn't feel like marketing." -Tom Fishburne

Monitoring and evaluation are often the most neglected parts of any plan. You need to create a plan to monitor and evaluate the success or failure of your plan.

For example, in terms of monitoring, make a list of things you're going to keep an eye on, to find out how well your marketing plan is working. For example:

- your blog's traffic, in terms of number of unique visitors daily
- number of queries you receive from prospective clients
- where prospective clients hear about you
- number of projects you receive per month

- number of bids you win from Elance or other bidding sites per month
- income you make per month

You should be able to know how you can get all this information. For instance, don't include "degree of prospects' liking and trust towards me" as something you will monitor, because you simply can't measure or observe that.

Set aside time, say every month, to go over these numbers to decide which of your marketing activities are really working. Then, regularly tweak and adjust your marketing plan until you reach your freelancing goals.

TIPS FOR MARKETING YOUR FREELANCE SKILLS gOOD

CHAPTER NINE

TRACK YOUR FREELANCING INCOME AND EXPENSES

"Don't freelance to make a living- freelance to make a life. Money is important- but when you hit ruts, work 16 hour days and get tough feedback, it's going to be something else that motivates you. You need to remember why you started and keep it in focus." Joel Klettke

Even if you're only freelancing part-time or as a sideline, you'll see many benefits from tracking your income and expenses, such as:

- You'll be able to see at a glance if you're really making money. You can easily tell how much money you're making, how much you're spending, and how much is left over.
- You'll be able to track the growth of your freelancing business.
- You can see which clients or types of services are bringing in most of your earnings.
- You and/or your accountant will have a much easier time when you file your income tax.

The 7
Principles
Agenda for a

KICKASS FREELANCE CAREER

Select Your Clients

Some clients don't get why you're charging more than $5. Stay away from them. It will harm your brand in the long term. Don't join the "race to the bottom" - it's hard to move away once you're in.

Learn To Sell

Doing the work is only half the battle. Learning how to present and sell your work and services is the other. Sales don't have to be sleazy, and learning to present your work in the best light is crutial.

Manage Your Time

Your projects need to be time-managed. Otherwise the work will take twice as much than expected. Use milestones and coordinate those with your client.

Understand Business

Learning how your client's business runs and works is the only way you can really solve their problems and add value.

Charge Your Worth

Just because you enjoy your work doesn't mean you should be charging pennies. Your work is a valuable business tool, charge accordingly.

Set Boundaries

In order to suceed in the long term, you need to set clear boundries with your clients. Perhaps you don't want to be bothered at 2am, or over WhatsApp.

Know Yourself

Understand your core strengths. And what your limitations are. And what you enjoy doing and what you hate. Then communicate those to your clients to find the best fit.

PROSPERO

www.goprospero.com

meditation icon by Pavel N. from the Noun Project

CHAPTER TEN
MISTAKES TO AVOID AS A FREELANCER

"No matter how much experience you have, how many degrees you have, or how well known you have become — there is always something new to learn. Don't rest on your past experiences. If you do nothing to improve your skills, you won't stay where you are." — Laura Spencer

Chances are, if you've been freelancing for a while you've made your fair share of mistakes. If you're a new freelancer, maybe you haven't made all the same mistakes *yet*, but you probably will before long. When working as a freelancer, there are some mistakes or common traps that can set you or your freelance business back, listed below are some mistakes to avoid:

1. Getting too comfortable
Getting too comfortable is a risk, you need to keep learning new things, tools and techniques to keep up with changing. Don't get too comfortable with where you are and what you are doing. It is important that you keep learning new things.

2. Working without a plan
As a freelancer you need to develop a business plan and strategy. Like where do you want to be in one year, five

years, or 20 years? If you are just working along with no regard to what comes next, you are in trouble. It will be hard to get there if you don't even know where you are going. You also need to have a financial, marketing plan tied to numbers. For example,

- Business revenue (How much do you need to make per month to live?)
- Site traffic (Where is it coming from? Whats your most popular content?)
- Link conversion rates and content interactivity (What calls-to-action are working? What pages arent getting views and need removed altogether?)

Knowing these numbers will shed light on the areas that need improvement.

3. Underestimating your work

One of the major problems with most new freelancers is that they severely undervalue their time and work. Doing projects for free or at very low cost, goes a long way in establishing what you are worth. Establish pricing that makes sense in your market and is in line with the services you offer and stick to it. Don't charge $50 for a project and charge $40 for that same project tomorrow except of course, you are giving bonus/discounts to clients. You can try out either a Time-Based Pricing, Project-Based Pricing or Value-Based Pricing.

5 MISTAKES

EVERY FREELANCER MAKES

avoid them in your career

NOT KNOWING WHEN TO SAY NO

You may be asked to work with a company with bad ethics. Or the client may add tasks to your current work pile. Sometimes "No" is necessary.

WORKING TOO MUCH

Thinking that you're the only one in your business sometimes makes you work every day, all day.

APPEALING TO EVERYONE

Focus and specialize in one or two services which could bring in more clients. Pick a niche that you love doing and something you're good at.

CHARGING TOO LITTLE

Actually has the opposite effect than you think. Clients may see you as 'cheap' and someone who provides low quality work.

HAVING NO FORMAL CONTRACT

Client may take advantage of this. You don't have to be a lawyer. Use one of the many templates available.

It's our human nature to make mistakes. If we didn't mess up once in a while, we would never learn. Don't feel bad.

Creative

4. Taking on every project that comes your way

Don't get stuck taking on every project that comes your way and either creating something that embarrasses you or that is overwhelming because you already have a full work load. Hence, it is important to know your own limits and strategically reject projects to make sure you can truly manage your workload. Successful freelancing is all about balance so you need to figure out what your standards are, set boundaries on what types of work and clients are best for you, and say no to projects that don't hit that bar. Always remember that when you say no to something, you are allowing yourself to use that block of time to say yes to something that makes sense and tally with your goal.

These are four projects to avoid:

- Projects that involves something you don't really know how to do.
- Projects from clients that don't actually know what they want or balk at paying from the start.
- Projects that give you an uncomfortable feeling. This can include anything from things you just don't believe in, have concerns about the legality of, and just don't feel like you can do well.
- Projects from family members or close friends are always tricky. It's hard to say no, but sometimes it

is the best thing so that feelings don't get hurt and relationships are not strained.

5. Getting too comfortable with your current clients

The truth about working as a freelancer is that any client could disappear any day. The solution is to expand your client base and ensure that you have good working relationships with your current clients. Some of it goes back to strategy as well. Do you have a plan for how to replace a client (and the coordinating revenue stream) if necessary?

6. No financial reporting system

Start tracking both your business expenses and income. At the beginning, you might not have a separate banking account for your personal and businesses finances. But it is ideal you set up something as simple as a spreadsheet or get an affordable accounting software to start recording your transactions. Failure to do this makes it difficult to develop an healthy financial habit with your freelance income.

7. Save your receipts

Avoid throwing receipts away. Tracking your income to know if you are earning enough to take care of yourself and build wealth is only possible when you track your business expenses so hold onto your receipts. When you have a freelance business, you can write off your business expenses on your taxes. Holding onto the receipts will organize and legitimize your records and make your taxes easier to complete.

CHAPTER ELEVEN
FINDING FREELANCE MARKETPLACES
FREELANCING JOBS

"Freelancers have allowed us to achieve things that would have been impossible otherwise" Beth Granai

Turn to your favorite search engine and search for some forums and databases specifically designed for freelancers seeking work in a particular field. There are tons of different places you can get work online, so within an hour or so you will probably have at least ten or fifteen places online where you can find employment as a freelancer.

Competing in Freelance Marketplaces

- **Be committed.** It takes time, energy and sometimes money (some sites charge a membership fee) to find quality freelancing jobs.

- **Be selective.** Don't waste your time competing with bottom feeders for low-paying assignments, or jobs you'd be miserable doing. Move on and keep looking.

- **Be persistent.** You'll win some, you'll lose some. Don't let a few disappointments stop you; your persistence will pay off.

- **Be flexible.** You may not be able to charge your published rates on Elance, but the network you create by gaining clients on Elance is worth it.
- **Be confident.** You're selling your services, so be unique and be bold with your offers but make sure you deliver on what you promise.

99designs

A platform for freelance designers, 99designs lets you compete in design contests and get feedback as clients choose the best ones. It's a great way for talented designers to prove their talents. 99designs welcomes freelance designers of all sorts, whether they specialize in advertising, merchandise, packaging, graphic work or illustration. Companies that are seeking freelance workers build a design brief, which 99designs launches as a prize-based contest open to its global network of designers in that category. Although only one freelancer will ultimately win, entering these contests is great practice and can help you build up your portfolio.

SriptLance

Those involved in the world of design and programming should turn to ScriptLance as their source of well-paying jobs in their chosen industry. As one of the leading websites for those involved in programming and design, this is probably the most likely place that you will find a well-paying job in the web and software field.

Freelance Job Search

If you are looking for other options, check out the Freelance Job Search, a website that will help you find lesser known, but well-paying freelance jobs in the world of web design, graphic design, and programming.

Aquent

Digital creative and marketing professionals can find work around the globe through Aquent staffing agency. You can choose from remote or on-site opportunities, and even look for contract-to-hire positions. The company also offers practical skills training through its free online courses, which can give freelancers a significant edge in the marketplace.

The Creative Group

The Creative Group specializes in job placement for professionals in creative fields like marketing, art, graphic design, copywriting, photography and more. While the listings include some contract-to-hire and full-time positions, you can use the "freelance" filter to narrow your search.

Crowded

Crowded simultaneously recruits independent workers and aggregates freelance job postings from hundreds of on-demand platforms to solve the supply-and-demand problems on both ends of the freelance equation. For freelancers, Crowded helps gather a wide variety of opportunities in one place, making it simple to find a steady stream of jobs.

CrowdSource

Crowdsource is one of the largest freelance work teams on the market, specializing in content creation, review and moderation for retailers, online publishers and media companies. The company breaks larger editorial tasks into micro tasks. Qualified freelancers can choose to work on these tasks through the website's WorkStation platform. If you perform well, you'll receive higher compensation and access to additional work.

Flexjobs

Flexjobs offers listings for part-time and freelance positions in more than 50 career tracks. The company hand screens each telecommuting job, so you can be sure that you're applying for a position with a legitimate company. Flexjobs also offers skills testing, job search tips and special members-only discounts through the site's partners.

Fiverr

Fiverr is a little different from your average freelance job-listing website. Instead of having companies post their projects so freelancers can apply, this site has freelancers create "gigs" based on what they're best at. That way, freelancers sell their services to the companies that find them. You can categorize your gig by keyword so it shows up in multiple searches.

Freelancer.com

The "world's largest outsourcing marketplace" offers freelancers several options for work, including project-based jobs, hourly work and contests. freelancer.com members can browse jobs that match their specific skill sets and apply to their chosen openings directly.

Guru

Like many freelance job websites, Guru displays a freelancer's portfolio, which includes reviews, past jobs and how much that person has earned through the site, so companies can verify the quality of a potential worker. The site also shows how much a particular company has spent on Guru Freelancers, so job seekers can make an educated decision about the companies they want to work for. Search for work by category, location and fixed versus hourly jobs.

Krop

A job-search board and portfolio builder in one place allows creative and tech professionals to put together personalized websites showcasing their skills to employers. The site features a mix of full-time, part-time and freelance work, searchable by location and keywords.

Peer Hustle

This recently launched app makes the process of finding and accepting jobs almost instantaneous. Like Uber, peer Hustle relies on geo location, meaning you're only competing with freelancers in your area for jobs posted by local companies. You can work remotely or in person, and communicate with potential clients in real time. Peer Hustle also guarantees that you'll be paid for a job well done: Your gig doesn't begin until the client funds an escrow account, which is released to you when your work meets the client's satisfaction.

Toptal

If you're a software developer, Toptal can help you find great work opportunities, fast. This marketplace puts all of its applicants through a series of screenings, tests and interviews and only accepts the top 3 percent of applicants. Because of this rigorous prescreening, potential employers know that members of Toptal's freelancer network are highly talented and ready to work immediately.

Upwork

With over 1.5 million clients, Upwork (previously oDesk) offers something for every type of freelancer. It accommodates both short- and long-term projects, hourly or per-project work and expert-level and entry-level engagements. Regardless of where you are in your career, Upwork is likely to have something for you. Upwork is a revamped, robust platform that connects companies with more than 10 million freelancers who are looking for contract jobs. From web and mobile development to writing, sales and marketing, design and consulting jobs. Freelancers can chat with potential and current clients, and accept or decline job opportunities directly within the Upwork mobile app. You can also display your "work status" to interested companies, which lets others know how quickly you can reply to job invitations.

FREELANCE INFOGRAPHIC

Freelancers statistics

UNITED STATES INDIA PAKISTAN UKRAINE UNITED KINGDOM
1   2   3   4   5

1 PERCENTAGE OF MEN AND WOMEN IN FREELANCING

100%
54%
46%

2 PERCENTAGE OF FREELANCERS EARNINGS IN THE WORLD

15-20%
53-60%
25-30%
0-1%

0-1%
5-10%
25-30%
50-60%

3 FREELANCERS PROFESSION

PROGRAMMER   DESIGNER   TRANSLATOR   WEB DEVELOPER   PHOTOGRAPHER   COPYWRITER

4 A PLACE TO WORK

5 WORK AND REST ANY TIME

Craigslist.com

Although most people see Craigslist as just a platform for buying and selling miscellaneous things, it's actually a great source of freelance jobs. You can easily browse for local offerings if you prefer something in-office, or you can search by major cities if you prefer working remotely.

Peopleperhour.com

This is a great platform, focusing on freelancing for web projects. If you're a designer, web developer, SEO specialist, etc., peopleperhour is definitely worth checking out..

DemandMedia.com

Demand Media is a platform for creative types, including writers, filmmakers, producers, photographers and more. You work with the site to create unique content, engage audiences and promote your talents.

CollegeRecruiter.com

As the name might suggest, College Recruiter is for college students or recent graduates looking for freelance jobs of any type. In addition to being a source for part-time work, it can be a great way to jumpstart your career.

GetACoder.com

This site is for freelance writers, web designers and programmers – exactly what small businesses need to get a website idea off the ground. GetACoder offers millions of smaller-scale projects to choose from.

iFreelance.com

This platform accommodates some of the usual suspects of the freelancing world (writers, editors, coders, etc.) but also features freelance marketers as well. Unlike other sites, iFreelance lets you keep 100 percent of your earnings.

Project4hire.com

With hundreds of project categories, Project4hire makes it easy to identify jobs that suit your skillset, without scanning through large volumes of posts. It's great for coders, consultants, designers and more.

SimplyHired.com

With a wider range than most other freelance platforms offer, SimplyHired is perfect for everyone from salespeople to construction workers. It includes a blog with hiring tips, a company directory and location-based search. Whether you're a programmer, designer, expert, college student or something in between, there's a freelance platform out there for you. Check out the sites above to get started today!

Other Great Websites To Get Freelancing Jobs

- Damongo.com
- DemandStudios.com
- Fourerr.com
- Findeavor.com
- FlexJobs.com
- Freelanced.com
- GenuineJobs.com
- Gigblasters.com
- Gigbucks.com
- Gigbux.com
- Gigdollars.com
- Greatlance.com
- HelpCove.com
- iFreelance.com
- IMGiGz.com
- JustAnswer.com
- JobBoy.com
- MechanicalTurk.com
- Microworkers.com
- Minijobz.com

- RapidWorkers.com
- ShortTask.com
- SmashingJobs.com
- Staff.com
- StudentFreelancing.com
- Taskr.com
- TenBux.com
- Tutor.com
- WeWorkRemotely.com
- Workhoppers.com
- YunoJuno.com
- Zeerk.com

Freelance Websites For Writers & Editors
- Freelance Writing Gigs
- Freelance Writing Jobs (Canadian)
- Government Bids
- Journalism Jobs
- Online Writing Jobs
- ProbloggerJobs.com
- RedGage.com
- Scribendi.com
- TaskArmy.com
- TextBroker.com
- Triond.com
- WriterBay.com

For Graphics Designers & computer Programmers:

- ArtWanted.com
- AuthenticJobs.com
- Behance.com
- ComputerAssistant.com
- CrowdSpring.com
- Coroflot.com
- DesignCrowd.com
- EnvatoStudio.com
- FieldNation.com
- Geniuzz.com
- GetACoder.com
- HexiDesign.com
- Joomlancers.com
- ProgrammerMeetDesigner.com
- Project4Hire.com
- SEOClerks.com
- Smashing Jobs.com
- TopCoder.com
- Toptal.com

CHAPTER TWELVE

PROS ANDS CONS OF FREELANCING

"Freelancing is tough. It can be very difficult, in fact. It can wear people down, making them lose sight of what they used to love because they have to do everything else just to get by." — *Mason Hipp*

PROS
1. More Flexible Hours
The first advantage of becoming a freelancer is that you can work whenever you want. You get to choose your own hours. If you want to sleep in until noon, you can do that. If you want to take the weekend off so you can explore the city, by all means, go for it. As a freelancer, you can actually work during your most productive hours, and those hours don't have to fall in during regular business hours.

2. You get to work wherever you want:
As a freelancer, you can choose to work from wherever you want .You are no longer stuck in an office or even in your home. Find a place in which you work best. You could work in a park, at the library, or in your living room.

3. You are your own boss

Freelancing gives you the chance to be in charge of the assignments you accept, you get to build the career that you want. Unlike an employee, you have the freedom of full control over the work you take on, and for whom you work. You no longer have to answer to anyone but your clients and yourself. You are free to do as you please, when you please. Making all the tough decisions just became your responsibility.

4. You Keep All the Profits

No longer do you have to work for a flat rate, no matter how large the projects are that you complete. Now, you get to allocate or keep all the profits from your large and small projects and clients. This gives you the freedom to then use that money to improve yourself and expand your business.

CONS

1. No Steady or Reliable Workloads

Unfortunately, being a freelancer means that your income and your workload are unstable and inconsistent. For the most part, you won't be able to depend on any regular project, client, or profit, whereas with a traditional job you always get an exact amount monthly.

2. Distinguishing between Work and Personal Time

Being your own boss and working from home or wherever you like also means that it can be difficult to distinguish between your work time and your personal life. This means that you can work long hours and never make time for your personal interests.

THE PROS AND CONS OF BEING A

Freelancer

There are 42 million freelancers in America. Lets see how freelancing is viable, or not.

SOME DO IT BY CHOICE.

Pros

COMPENSATION 45%

The Average freelancer makes 45% more than your normal worker.

$68,000 VS. $46,800

75% of those who work from home make over **$65,000** per year

(80TH PERCENTILE EARNINGS)

49% of freelancers earn $20-$59/ hr.

33% of freelancers earn $70+/ hr.

15% of freelancers earn $100+/ hr.

BALANCE Freelancers have great work life balance. They can take yoga breaks whenever.

Only **29%** of N. American freelancers work 40+ hours a week.

OTHERS DO IT BECAUSE THERE IS NO CHOICE.

Cons

PESSIMISM 21%

say they are moderately or very much unhappier than at a traditional job.

Top COMPLAINTS

(by percent of freelancers claiming something was their "biggest challenge.")

20.8% Finding clients

16.3% Feast or famine cycle

10.1% Maintaining work life balance

3. Not Getting Paid

Being a freelancer also means that you run the risk of not getting paid. This is fairly common in the freelance world, and one more hat you'll have to wear is that of a debt collector. There are ways to protect yourself from non-paying clients, but sometimes you won't realize you're at risk until it's too late.

4. No Employer Benefits

Health benefits are expensive. Depending on your current health, switching to a freelance lifestyle might not be in your best interest. Also, starting your own freelance business means you no longer have paid sick days or vacation time to use. Every day you don't work is a day you won't get paid.

CHAPTER THIRTEEN

TECH TOOLS FOR FREELANCING

"Freelancing involves surviving on your wits and talent."
Marianne Gray

Every business, especially solo operations like freelancing, needs the right tools to run effectively. As a new freelancer, you may not think of yourself as a business owner, but in reality, that is exactly what you are. You are marketing your services be it writing, graphic design, photography, proof reading etc. to various companies and getting paid for your time and effort. You're filling out invoices and tax forms, and keeping your portfolio updated for prospective clients, just like many other types of small businesses. Whether you're freelancing full time or just doing a side project or two for extra income, here are some tech tools that can help you manage your business better.

Online Portfolios

Whether you're an artist, photographer, designer, as a creative professional, your website is often a potential client's initial point of contact with you and your best chance to create that all-important first impression.

If you are just starting out, you might not have an extensive portfolio of sample pieces. Eventually, though, you will need a way to showcase existing work on your website.

However, there are free and premium WordPress portfolio and gallery plugins available that enable you to easily add a portfolio section to your existing website.

Why you need a WordPress portfolio plugin

There are WordPress themes available with built in portfolio capabilities, but if you're happy with your current theme, it makes sense to install a portfolio plugin rather than changing themes.

Plus, plugins make it easy to manage and display your portfolio in a professional manner from a central location within WordPress. The terms **gallery** and **portfolio** plugin are often used interchangeably. However, a gallery plugin is more suitable for image-centric pieces like photographs, and a strict portfolio plugin works best for projects with additional details. Below, are some examples of plug ins you can use for your portfolios

1. Nimble Portfolio

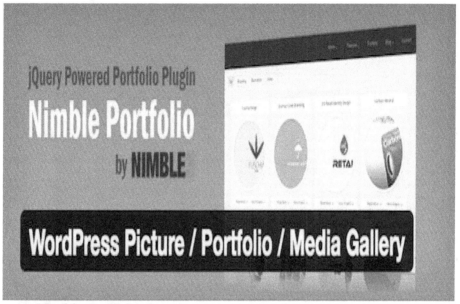

Nimble Portfolio features a responsive layout ensuring a professional look on both desktop and mobile devices. The built-in PrettyPhoto lightbox attractively displays a variety of media types like photos, videos and even PDFs.

Thumbnails are easily styled and customizable, and built-in categorization and sorting features enable visitors to quickly browse through specific areas of your portfolio.

Add New Portfolio Item

Nimble Portfolio Example

Publish ▾

📷 Add Media   Visual   Text

B *I* ᴬᴮᶜ ☰ ☰ 66 – ☰ ☰ ☰ 𝒫 ✂ ☰   ⋯

🖼 🖼

This is an example of a client portfolio item.

Filters ▴

Filters   Most Used

☑ Pets

+ Add New Filter

Featured Image ▴

Word count: 9   Draft saved at 5:51:44 pm.

Remove featured image

Options ▴

Image/Video URL

URL from Media Library

Enter URL for the full-size image or video (youtube, vimeo, swf, quicktime) you want to display in the lightbox gallery. You can also choose Image URL from your Media gallery (Please note: If this field is empty then Featured Image will be used in lightbox gallery)

Portfolio URL

http://example.com/

Enter URL to the live version of the project

The free version of Nimble Portfolio is impressive, but the developer also offers premium add-ons that include different skins, lightboxes and alternate sorting capabilities.

2. Essential Grid ($26)

Essential Grid is a powerful plugin from ThemePunch, the development team responsible for Slider Revolution.

ThemePunch claims that Essential Grid is "the most popular grid plugin for WordPress". First impressions are great. The plugin's site shows off a variety of examples, ranging from artistic portfolios to WooCommerce products to social media streams.

Using the plugin is easy – you're just embedding a shortcode into a post or page. The powerful configuration options are handled in the WordPress admin. You create each grid and walk through each tab – Source, Grid Settings, Skins, Animations, et al. – to customize the grid.

One of the most powerful features is the ability to edit the "skin" (appearance) of tiles, or items, in a grid. The Item Skin editor provides a drag-and-drop UX to customize everything. You don't need to know any CSS.

3. Wonder Portfolio Grid

The Wonder Portfolio Grid plugin is a freemium plugin packed with features. You can create multiple galleries; an overlay to portfolio items; filter items by category; click into a variety of media (audio, video, images); open media in a lightbox; handle captions; integrate with social media; and use multiple layouts.

The free version doesn't limit features, but images are watermarked. The paid upgrade costs $80. Considering the time you would save on custom development, though, that's a great price!

4. NextGEN Gallery

With more than a million active installs, NextGEN Gallery is the most popular WordPress gallery plugin – a perfect fit for photographers.

You can create, manage and organize photo galleries, and group them into albums. Photos can be tagged, cropped, watermarked and have metadata added to them – either individually or in batch mode.

Gallery : NextGEN Gallery Example

Gallery settings (Click here for more settings)

Title:	NextGEN Gallery Example	ⓘ Link to page:	Not linked ▾
Description:		Preview image:	[1] cat-914110_1920.jpg ▾
Gallery path:	/wp-content/gallery/nextgen-gal	Create new page:	Main Page (no parent) ▾ Add page
Author	Tom Ewer		

Scan Folder for new images   Save Changes

Bulk actions ▾   Apply   Sort gallery   Save Changes   Images per page: 50 ▾ 6 items

☐	ID	Thumbnail	Filename	Alt & Title Text / Description	Tags
☐	1		cat-914110_1920.jpg October 21, 2015 1920 x 1279 pixels ☐ Exclude ?	cat	
			View Meta Edit thumb Rotate Publish Recover Delete		
☐	2		guinea- pig-498848_1920.jpg	guinea pig	

NextGEN gallery is fully responsive and images can be displayed in either a slideshow, thumbnail or single-photo style with multiple types of lightbox effects available to choose from.

The free version is powerful and will be enough for most users. If you require support or additional features and options like a masonry layout or filmstrip galleries, NextGEN sells a premium Plus version and a Pro version with integrated e-commerce capabilities.

5. Envira Gallery Lite

The full Envira Gallery is a premium plugin ranging in price from $19 to $249 depending on features and support. In this case we are looking at the free, trimmed-down Envira Gallery Lite. The Lite version lacks certain features such as add-ons and advanced customizability, but it is more than suitable for photographers and artists who need a simple, easy-to-configure gallery plugin.

This plugin's support for additional details is limited, so designers would be better off with a more project-focused portfolio plugin.

Envira Gallery Lite is mobile-responsive and uses images from your WordPress website's media library. Various cropping, layout, and multi-column display options are also available.

Galleries are added to pages through a WordPress shortcode and, on the front end, clicking a thumbnail opens the image in a basic lightbox. Additional styles and options are available in the full Envira Gallery plugin.

3. Media Grid

Media Grid is a premium gallery plugin. With approximately 9,000 sales and a 4.5-star rating based on over 700 reviews (at the time of this writing) it's evident that Media Grid is tremendously popular. Like many plugins sold at CodeCanyon, it bundles a visual grid builder, enabling easy drag-and-drop gallery building, sorting and resizing.

You will also find various lightbox and display styles, a built-in media player, grid pagination (multiple pages), WooCommerce product integration, integrated item search, nearly unlimited customization options, and much more besides.

A handy feature worth mentioning, Media Grid enables the user to define unique item characteristics – attributes – that can be used to create an entirely custom portfolio.

7. WordPress Portfolio Plugin (WP Portfolio)

WP Portfolio is a free WordPress plugin suitable for web designers and writers. It uses the free Shrink The Web service to automatically generate screenshots of your published online work, or alternatively, you can use self-created images.

This plugin doesn't include fancy lightbox effects or gallery features; it presents your items in a simple, directory-style layout. The default look is basic yet functional and the appearance can be customized with CSS and HTML.

Add New Website Details

Website Name	WP Portfolio Example
	The proper name of the website. *(Required)*
Website URL	http://example.com
	The URL for the website, including the leading *http://*. *(Required)*
Website Description	This is a sample description about the website.
	The description of your website. HTML is permitted. *(Required)*
Website Group	My Websites ▾
	The group you want to assign this website to.

Show Advanced Settings

[Add Website Details]

Configuration is performed in the WordPress backend. To display your portfolio on your website, just add a shortcode to any new or existing WordPress page.

8. Easy Portfolio

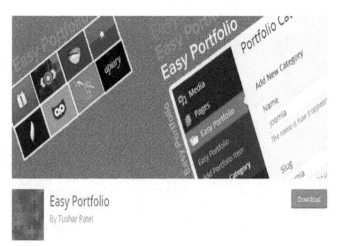

Easy Portfolio
By Tushar Patel

Download

Easy Portfolio is a lightweight plugin for adding portfolios to your website. Portfolio entries are saved as a custom post type and organized with a custom taxonomy. Using a short code, you can embed portfolio galleries on any post or page.

Customize the embedded portfolios by specifying the number of portfolio items and the categories you want to pull from. Easy Portfolio is a good solution if you're looking for basic functionality without much fuss.

9. Gallery by GhozyLab

Gallery – Responsive Image Gallery Plugin

By Gallery Team - GhozyLab

Download

The Gallery plugin by GhozyLab is another free, lightweight portfolio plugin for WordPress.

Unlike the Easy Portfolio plugin, this plugin includes a bunch of features: support for image galleries; photo albums; image carousels & sliders; audio; video; even Google Maps.

You can even upgrade to a Pro version, which unlocks more customization and styling features, plus additional documentation and 24/7 support.

10. Go Portfolio ($29)

Go Portfolio is a premium WordPress portfolio plugin. While Go Portfolio is compatible with any WordPress theme (just embed it on a post or page), it's compatibility with Visual Composer is called out in particular.

The layout is responsive and customizable. It supports unlimited portfolios and unlimited custom post types, including querying post types to populate the portfolio.

As with many premium portfolio plugins, Go Portfolio also includes support for WooCommerce, so you can load your portfolio with purchasable products.

And finally, the plugin is well reviewed, with an average rating of 4.59 out of 5 stars.

11. WP Auto Grid ($18)

WP Auto Grid is another premium WordPress plugin, but unlike Go Portfolio, it takes a different approach to how items are managed.

Instead of creating a custom post type and having you add items through the WordPress admin, you point WP Auto Grid to a folder within your WordPress installation that contains images. WP Auto Grid scans the folder and ingests the images as gallery entries. Any sub-folders are treated as categories within the gallery.

Why would you want this sort of functionality? Imagine you've got hundreds of photos sitting on a hard drive. Manually importing all of those photos as separate gallery entries would be exhausting. If you wanted to automate the process, you'd need to write some custom code to do it for you.

WP Auto Grid is perfect for that scenario. And when you're building (or re-building) an image-heavy website, like a portfolio, it's a boon to your productivity.

OTHER TECH TOOLS

1. Organization and Project Management

- **Basecamp**

It is typically used by teams, but this Web-based project management software can be very useful for freelancers who want to keep clients in the loop about ongoing projects. With unlimited users for each package level, you can invite any of your clients to view your Basecamp and get details on your progress with their tasks. You can also determine which users have access to individual projects, so your clients will see only what's relevant to them.

- **Dropbox**

Every freelancer needs a reliable file-sharing and Cloud storage solution Whether you need to back up and store data, share documents or collaborate on projects, a cloud service like Dropbox lets you access your files anytime, anywhere there is an Internet connection using your computer or mobile device.

- **Wunderlist**

Staying organized is key to a freelancer's success. Wunderlist is a simple, intuitive to-do list app that can be accessed on your desktop or mobile devices for free. To-dos can be organized by project and by client, and then broken down by tasks needed to complete each item. Additional features include the ability to add notes and files (such as photos and spreadsheets) to each to-do item, set deadlines, and create reminders and automatic data syncing across all devices.

- **Trello**

Say goodbye to sticky notes, disorganized calendars and overwhelming to-do lists with Trello. This project management tool lets you keep track of ideas, to-do lists, things currently in progress and completed tasks using a virtual, Pinterest-like whiteboard. Each item is set up as a "card" that you can drag and drop within and across categories, making it easy to organize projects and your entire freelance business. Start using Trello with a free account.

2. Time Management

- **My Minutes**

It is an iOS app that helps you meet productivity goals by budgeting your time. It uses an "at least" and "at most" system, such as "spending at least two hours on Client A's project" and "spending at most an hour on emails." The app can also send daily notifications of your to-do list, as well as motivate you with alerts when you have reached a goal or are close to hitting one. My Minutes can be downloaded for free from the Apple App Store.

- **Rescue Time**

If you're billing by the hour, it is critical to understand how you're spending your time. **RescueTime** works in the background of your computer or mobile device, tracking the amount of time you spend on applications and websites, as well as time spent away from your desk.

- **Toggl**

Another useful time tracking software for freelancers is **Toggl**, a Web-based software that allows you to easily create, start and stop timers for tasks with a single click. You can categorize timed tasks by client, add tags and mark them as "billable," which also serves to keep you organized when you're juggling multiple projects. The basic version of Toggl is free and gives you unlimited projects and detailed reports of your time.

3. Accounting

- **Harvest**

Take the guesswork out of billing clients. **Harvest** offers an all-in-one solution that both tracks time and does all the number-crunching for you. In addition to one-click time tracking— simply click Start when you begin and Stop when you've finished — Harvest can automatically generate invoices based on time worked, log and analyze expenses, create professional-looking estimates and more.

- **FreshBooks**

Simplify your accounting system with this cloud-based accounting software system for non-accountants. It not only tracks billable hours, but also integrates them with an easy online invoicing system that automatically calculates totals and taxes to quickly generate invoices. FreshBooks also offers hassle-free expense tracking that automatically imports and categorizes expenses from bank accounts and credit cards, and it logs expenses simply by taking a snapshot of receipts.

Its financial reporting tools include expense reports, quarterly analysis, profits and losses, payments collected, tax summaries and more.

- **Zoho Books**

As Business News Daily's pick for best micro-business accounting software, Zoho Books is an ideal solution for freelancers who want a simple, un-cluttered approach to accounting. It allows you to create and send invoices, track expenses, sync your bank accounts and create reports on the Web or via its mobile app. While it's a bit higher priced than other accounting solutions, at $24 a month (after a free 14-day trial), Zoho Books gives you the best bang for your buck by including access to all of its features, plus unlimited everything.

4. Business Operations
- **EchoSign**

Signing contracts, proposals, agreements and other types of paperwork is a significant part of being a freelancer. EchoSign, Adobe's secure electronic signature solution, lets freelancers use any Web browser or mobile device to send and e-sign documents, eliminating the time wasted in printing, signing, scanning and sending files. EchoSign also features tracking capabilities when documents are viewed and signed, and works with popular file formats like Word, PDF, Excel, PowerPoint and more.

CHAPTER FOURTEEN

MAKING A CHOICE

"The strongest principle of growth lies in human choice"-
George Eliot

After exploring what freelancing entails, how to go about it, market your skill successfully and starting with some leverage, you might still be uncertain as to whether it is the right career path for you. Well, the ball really lies in your court!

Like I emphasized, it would be great for you to try freelancing part time, get a few clients and then determine if it is something you want to do in the long run. Also remember that even if you are totally sure that you want to become a freelancer in your chosen field, you have to look at how possible it is for you financially?

If you currently do not even have a job and you are contemplating freelancing with your skills or learning one or two skills and then go into freelancing, here are a few points you can use in assessing how well you will fit.

"Some of our important choices have a time line. If we delay a decision, it is gone forever. Sometimes our doubts keep us from making a choice that involves change. Thus an opportunity may be missed."

James E. Faust

- Can you support yourself on the salary you make from a freelancer? What about healthcare, are you prepared to give that up too in pursuit of a future as a freelancer? Without the support of an already established business behind you, you will have to pay for your own (and your family's) health insurance out of pocket.

 This is not a big deal if you have a spouse that gets health insurance from his or her workplace, but if your spouse is a stay at home parent or is involved in their own freelance business, this becomes a major expense to think about. So be sure that you will be able to afford health insurance for all of your loved ones when you become a freelancer.

- Can you handle the stress that comes from working with tight, often ridiculous deadlines on your projects? Stress management is a key factor of working for you as a freelancer. You will be faced with projects that may require you to work long and hard before you can finish them.
Often, these projects will be extremely difficult and be under some ludicrous deadline – making them that much more intense. So, are you good at handling stressful situations such as these?
After all, if you are not able to get the project back to your client on time and in working order, you may be discredited and have a much more difficult time finding work for many months to come.

> Freedom is realizing you have a choice.
>
> *T.F. Hodge*

- Do you work well by yourself and can you speak well when talking with a potential client who may want to hire you for his next project?

- Do you have what it takes to constantly advertise yourself and your services to anyone who may be interested? Do you have enough self esteem that you can promote yourself as if you are the best freelancer out there? Being able to constantly advertise your services is a major benefit for anyone looking to become a freelancer.

  While it is possible to by shy or withdrawn and be successful at freelancing, you will have a much easier time if you are more vocal about promoting your services to prospective customers.

- You have to figure out whether or not you can support your family on the salary you will make as a freelancer. Remember that you will have to take a pay cut from your current job when you first start out as a freelancer, and when you finally quit your current job for good, will you be able to bring in enough work to keep your family's lifestyle at the same level it currently is?

- Are you a team player or do you work better as an individual? While this question may seem insignificant, remember that as a freelancer you really have no team to rely on should you not know how to do something.

Sure, you could scour the internet for answers to your questions – but that will take away valuable time from your project. So, if you are the type of

person who can accomplish tasks more efficiently in a group, then you may want to rethink the idea of going freelance, because the individualize work environment of a freelancer is certainly not for you.

These are important questions that you have to ask yourself before you make that big leap into the world of freelancing. Far too often, people think that they want to be freelancers simply because it sounds cool. Many people get it into their heads that there is no more relaxing work atmosphere than being able to wake up late, work on your computer while you are wearing your pajamas and take off whatever days you want as your vacation.

Sure, those are all perks of being a freelancer, but let's be honest here - there are quite a few trials and tribulations that you will have to go through as a freelancer before you can reach the point where you do not have to worry about your finances anymore.

Yes, that is something that so many people fail to realize – you cannot expect to simply quit your current job for life as a freelancer and suddenly have hundreds of potential clients knocking at your door in hope that you will do a project for them.

There is much more to freelancing than that, so let's find out if you have what it takes to make it in the cutthroat world of the freelancer. You have to realize that you may not be able to make ends meet on freelancing alone for quite some time. So, if you are thinking about quitting your current job – don't do it just yet. Instead, test the waters and be sure that you like freelancing first, and find out how much money you can make as a freelancer before you even begin to work on your resignation papers.

As a fledgling freelancer, your best bet is to start off with clients that may not pay as much but will be able to get you in the door. Sure, you will have to take jobs that you may think are below you – but trust me, in the end it will pay off. Maybe not financially at first, but by way of getting your name out there and adding employment opportunities to your ever expanding list of satisfied customers. Therefore, if you want to freelance professionally, you have to be willing to take a pay cut at first in order to be successful later.

While it is not very important if you decide to keep doing freelance work as a supplement to your current income – it will become extremely important if you decide to make your freelance salary your sole income.

Freelancing is hard — make sure it's right for you. In the end, no path is right for everyone. Yes, freelancing offers more choices, but it also comes with more responsibilities. There are any number of tasks and demands that get overlooked when working for someone else. Consider who you are, what your current needs and goals are, and decide if you want to take on the challenges of freelancing.

Remember, having a skill isn't enough to create a successful business, but if you're willing and able to take on these new responsibilities, you can have the opportunity to shape your own future.

Stephen Akintayo, an inspirational speaker and Serial Entrepreneur is currently the Chief Executive Officer of Stephen Akintayo Consulting International and Gtext Media and Investment Limited, a leading firm in Nigeria whose services span from Digital Marketing, Website Design, Bulk SMS, Online Advertising, Media, E-Commerce, Real Estate, Consulting and a host of other services.

Stephen, Also Founded GileadBalm Group Services which has assisted a number of businesses in Nigeria to move to enviable levels by helping them reach their clients through its enormous nationwide data base of real phone numbers and email addresses. It has hundreds of organizations as its clients including multinational companies like Guarantee Trust Bank, PZ Cussons, MTN, Chivita, among others.
Stephen, popularly called Pastor Stephen is also the founder of Omonaija, an online radio station and SAtv in Lagos currently streaming for 24 hours daily with the capacity to reach every country of the world.

To invite **Stephen Akintayo** for a speaking engagement kindly visit

stephenakintayo.com/bookings
email: invite@stephenakintayo.com or
call: 0818 811 1999

www.ingramcontent.com/pod-product-compliance
Lightning Source LLC
La Vergne TN
LVHW022319060326
832902LV00020B/3557